BE YOUR OWN BLACKSMITH: THE CRAFT OF BUILDING YOURSELF

DR. JIPSON THOOMKUZHY

COPYRIGHT PAGE

This is a non-fiction work. All the characters, organizations, and events portrayed in this book are either product of the author's experience or knowledge.

BE YOUR OWN BLACKSMITH: THE CRAFT OF BUILDING YOURSELF

ISBN: 978-93-342-3891-4

DEDICATION

This book is lovingly dedicated to a select few individuals who have played an immensely significant role in shaping my life. Though two of them have departed from this world, their memories continue to guide me. First and foremost, I dedicate this book to my paternal grandfather, who patiently taught me to write my first letter in Malayalam on a slate crafted from metamorphic rock. Your boundless love and wisdom have left an indelible mark on my heart. May your soul find eternal peace and everlasting joy in Paradise. To my mother, whose unconditional love nurtured and shaped me into the person I am today. Your values and unwavering support have been my guiding light through life's challenges. May you find eternal tranquility and endless happiness in Paradise. Though your time with us was brief, your memory will forever live on in my heart. I love you and miss you beyond measure. To my father, who stood by me, loved me unconditionally, and instilled the principles of hard work and perseverance. Your guidance and strength have been my pillars of support, lifting me above life's obstacles. Without you, I would be lost in this world.

Furthermore, I express my heartfelt gratitude to my beloved spouse, devoted son, cherished daughter, and the Almighty God for their unwavering encouragement and support throughout the challenging journey of completing this book. Your unconditional love has been my constant source of inspiration, propelling me forward at every step of this extraordinary endeavor. With love, appreciation, and eternal gratitude.

PREFACE

Inside every person is a spark, a small, quiet flame of potential. Life brings the heat. It brings the pressure, the challenges, and the changes. What happens next is up to you. Some give in to fear or doubt. Others step forward, ready to grow. This book is for those who choose to step forward.

Growth isn't fast. It doesn't come with shortcuts or loud applause. It comes with effort. With patience, like a blacksmith at work, shaping metal in the fire, you shape who you become through choices, habits, and how you handle pressure. Real strength doesn't appear all at once. It's built over time. This book is a guide for that journey. Each part follows a natural path of personal growth: discovering your purpose, building confidence, creating discipline, bouncing back from setbacks, forming strong values, leading with heart, and committing to lifelong learning. Every chapter gives you tools, not just ideas. Each one is meant to help you take clear steps forward.

The forge is a symbol in this book, not just for heat, but for transformation. You won't find perfect answers here. What you will find is real guidance for real life. The goal is not perfection, it's progress. It's showing up, even when things are tough. It's making choices that match who you want to become. This book is for anyone in motion starting a fresh, rebuilding, or just trying to move forward. Whether facing a tough season or chasing a new dream, the journey is the same: keep showing up. Growth doesn't happen in one big moment it happens in the small ones you repeat daily.

Let these words remind you that you're not stuck. You're being shaped. You're not too late. You're still becoming. And that matters.

So step in. Pick up the tools. Trust the fire.

This is your forge.

This is where your growth begins.

CONTENTS

CHAPTER 1

IGNITING THE FIRE WITHIN YOUR INNER MOTIVATION

INTRODUCTION

Small thoughts must occur inside your brain before considering any action, making a significant decision, or achieving substantial goals. "*The whole battle for victory is won or lost in the mind.*"The world will tell you that your job, relationship, or life stages fuel your motivation. However, that is untrue. The thing is, motivation has to come from within you. It is not only cultivated but also developed.

The grim truth is that motivation is not one-off. It is not a spark that catches Fire and instantly goes off. It is a flame and must be kept burning. You cannot just set Fire and anticipate it to persist. *"You must add a stoker, guard it, and fuel it daily.*" People miss their objectives because they lack the desired skills, rather than having the motivation levels. External elements, such as doubts, distractions, and uncertainties from the world, can extinguish the flame. "*Your objectives succeed when they link directly with your most passionate values.*"

The key to real achievement lies in starting and sustaining your inner motivation throughout the challenging course of your task. Before teaching sustainability methods for your Fire, you must examine the spark-finding process. You should evaluate "*Which steps help you to locate your internal forces for self-activation?*" The initial requirement for success involves recognizing your identity and determining your driving forces. Once you uncover your inner motivation, you discover your authentic potential, as outlined in this chapter, which explains the path to revealing it.

1.1 THE SPARK: DISCOVERING WHAT DRIVES YOU

There are moments in which the dreams happen, and the spark begins in an individual when that individual tries to feel that dream. You need to define the core basis of your success: *is it promotion, beating the competition, or any other such achievements?* Let's be frank. Most people never find their true motivation. They live their lives according to the expectations of others without pausing to consider the question, "*What truly drives me?*" You can set yourself apart from the others at this point.

Discovering your flame is something you actively seek out; it doesn't just happen. It's about *self-awareness, self-reflection, and, most importantly, clarity.* Have you ever wondered how to locate your source of motivation? The path to success turns out to be simpler than anticipated. "*You must find a way back to the moment that brought the most focus, intense energy, and deep involvement.*" No matter what you do in life, people will always have something to say, so it is advisable to refine your opinions and feedback to find the genuine ones that will help you succeed.

"*You need to start to listen to yourself.*" Your search for approval from others should come to an end, and you should prioritize it based on your wisdom, without considering society's views on the value of life. The journey toward personal motivation requires discarding expectations that come from outside influence. Think about the last time you had control of creating something that flows from your core values. Your spark exists so that you can start building the Fire within your heart.

Oprah Winfrey was told that she was *'unfit for TV'* and she was fired from her early job as a television reporter. Instead of giving up on her dreams, she listened to something more profound: the spark within that made her feel alive, drawing her to the story and connection. That quiet pull helped her create "*The Oprah Winfrey Show*" and, with it, a career and an inspirational legacy. Similarly, Steve Jobs also dropped out of college and wandered until a calligraphy class provoked an intense interest in design and aesthetics. That small interest became the building blocks of Apple's revolutionary user experience. Both stories show that the spark isn't always dramatic. It needs to be a quiet moment of clarity where you rediscover what you love.

Discovering your life's motivation marks the beginning of a new chapter in your existence. Motivation is only one piece among many aspects you need to pursue. The source will direct your selection of options, behavioral actions, and life's direction. Your spark should shape your decisions. It should guide your behavior, choices, and long-term objectives. You should be moving forward with a purpose. You will no longer excuse yourself, and that spark is enough to drive you. So go ahead, "*find your spark.*" It is out there just waiting for you to discover it, and once you get hold of it, there is nothing a person can do to postpone it.

1.2 EMOTIONAL ALCHEMY: TURNING PAIN INTO POWER

Life lacks straightforwardness due to its winding course. Your journey toward achieving your dreams includes numerous barriers, including rejections, failures, disappointments, and setbacks. The reality that people rarely acknowledge is that pain serves as your driving force rather than your opposition. All successful people have endured painful experiences while developing their capabilities through these traumatic events. "*When you become motivated, you learn not to let pain push you back but instead push you forward.*"

Rethink the most difficult challenge you have experienced, and you may have experienced failure in an essential matter. Some individuals would have even told you that you lack skills. Don't get disappointed. "*The reality of failure stands clear because it signals the start of your development journey.*" The beginning of your personal development commences at that moment. A significant personal crisis would rock your foundations, but you must encounter it. "*The situation had the power to defeat you, but you must transform into a new perspective.*" Your experience of facing challenging circumstances has enabled you to develop superior capabilities. The setback becomes your drive to study diligently while developing better self-improvement skills.

Throughout our life experiences, pain functions as a central source of knowledge. Assessing your weaknesses becomes necessary because being willing to learn from your shortcomings will result in better personal growth. "*One of the amazing capabilities of emotional alchemy is that it lets you convert intense, difficult emotional sensations into beneficial outcomes*." Your strength increases with every encounter of pain that you manage to overcome. You become more resilient and more driven.

After overcoming what she experienced as a child, Maya Angelou (Iconic American Poet) might have let her pain become her only story. She transformed it into poetry, prose, and strong advocacy for causes, enabling her ideas to reach millions. What made her strong was what she had gone through. J.K. Rowling suffered depression and hardship as a single mom, but her writing turned that hardship into a series full of hope. From what they went through, it is clear that turning pain into power is possible. It is prioritized building strength by working through your experiences and creating a bigger, brighter, more human story.

The idea is that you should not avoid pain because you need to be open to it. Each impediment that comes your way allows you to develop and build knowledge and master your craft. A different perception of pain allows you to disengage from its influence. Taking control of pain will make you stronger as opposed to becoming the victim of your problems. You must explore opportunities to turn each obstacle into a moment to discover fresh ideas, as significant accomplishments often emerge following intense challenges. When life presents challenges, you should not shy away from them; instead, welcome them, as they provide knowledge that drives your pursuit of goals. "*Finding enduring strength from temporary pain becomes a permanent asset.*"

1.3 THE MOTIVATION MAP: CHARTING YOUR PATH TO PASSION

The Motivation map is about learning to navigate by what fuels you. You should focus this desire on achieving your objectives after identifying your motivation and turning hardship into a source of strength. "*A motivational flame without a goal works like an undirected fire.* It will exhaust itself, so a map is necessary. You must have a plan. Specific action items in your plan should guide your progressive movement. When everyday life takes over without clear direction, it's easy to lose motivation.

Motivation alone cannot sustain an individual because the absence of direction causes Fire to diminish, even with abundant fuel. Your path and vector (direction) are essential in your journey. You require information about your destination and the path that leads to it. You must use a properly designed motivation map to convert your dreams into life success. You need to establish quantitative targets to divide into compact operational tasks. Your descriptions become precise, making your route more exact.

The essential requirement is that your goals must contain concrete steps for execution. Merely wanting to become successful is insufficient. Does success have a particular vision in your mind? To pursue a marathon run, you need to specify your goal: "*I will exercise thrice weekly to develop my endurance until I reach six months of training.*" Such goals require precise action steps for implementation. It's measurable and it is specific. When you break down your goal into small increments, each portion enables you to maintain forward momentum. "*Momentum is your secret weapon.*" It is the force that keeps you moving. The feeling of forward motion fuels your confidence, and it keeps you engaged.

Steven Spielberg's journey to becoming a movie director was marked by repeated failures when he tried to get into film school. Instead of giving up, he moved forward, and he felt that closed doors led him to even better options. He continued to explore every little idea, making short films as a teenager and using new jobs to become involved in movies like Jaws and E.T. Similarly, Serena Williams achieved greatness in tennis because she worked hard, believed in herself, and followed her childhood goals. From what we learn, passion does not strike us overnight; it develops gradually if we are patient and brave. The motivation map focuses on identifying what inspires you, what challenges you, and what fills your life with energy. Then, you can use that knowledge to chart the right path for the future.

A written plan should remain adaptable because life changes persistently. Expected life events may not always unfold as planned, as obstacles are bound to arise during your journey. That's where flexibility comes in. "*Your motivation map acts as a flexible guide that adapts to the present situation alongside all your life movements.*"The adjustment of your map happens during your path of progress. The solution to challenges emerges through a combination of transformation and education, along with ongoing progress. Any temporary failures function as a redirection in your life. When you stay consistently focused on your destination, your motivation will propel you forward, even in the face of obstacles.

1.4 THE FORGE OF DREAMS: VISUALIZING YOUR IDEAL FUTURE

Visualizing your future is more than just daydreaming; it's a potent tool that helps you focus, change your perspective, and determine how to go. Let's discuss the future and visualize it. Close your eyes and imagine your ideal future in five years or ten. "*Visualization is imagining, feeling, tasting, smelling, and experiencing a sense of achievement in your mind before it happens.*" Your likelihood of achieving your ideals in the real world arises from the details of your Visualization.

Visualize your mind as a forge. When you focus on your dreams, you turn them into something, heating them until they cannot be just ideas anymore. We should know what we want to accomplish when we start our journey. The idea of fulfillment, the happiness of overcoming difficulties, and the pride of victory are the things that we have to imagine. That vision should take root in your heart, and that inspirational leverage should light your path.

Getting lost in the daily routine and losing sight of the larger view is easy. And when you consistently imagine your perfect future, you attach yourself to what you want to do. It is a compass, guiding you the whole way and keeping it constant to show you the route you should take. But the thing is: "*Visualization is not idleness. It requires an emotional connection.*" You must not only envision the dream but sense it. Just think of the thrill, the motivation, and the accomplishment you will feel once you accomplish what you want to do. You fire up your motivation when you align with your emotions and vision.

Visualization by itself is not enough. You can't just sit there and hope for change to occur; change has to occur throughout your life; it doesn't happen through mere wishes. Visualization needs to be combined with action.

The more defined your vision is, the more emotional it becomes, and the more it inspires you to take action to make that vision a reality. You are not just dreaming of success. You are mentally getting ready to meet it halfway with action. Keep that vision in your mind daily; it will become the spark that keeps your Fire burning.

As a child, when Beyoncé was not yet a global pop icon, she would stand and stare at herself in a mirror, picturing herself performing onstage to thousands of, picturing the crowd, the lights, the sound, the feeling. That was not just a fantasy, but a blueprint for reality. She stepped in, choosing how to piecemeal her dream into destiny. In much the same way, Jim Carrey, an American Canadian actor, wrote a post-dated check for $10 million to himself for acting services rendered and dated it five years into the future. He had it in his wallet and pictured it successfully until the film "*Dumb and Dumber*" became famous. Analyzing these stories, belief and clarity are the driving forces behind the forging of dreams. When you dare to vividly imagine your dream future, you start shaping it because of what your mind rehearses; your heart begins to chase, and that world starts to respond accordingly.

The most successful people in the world, from athletes to entrepreneurs, use this visualization technique. They do not just imagine success. They embody it. "*The mind does not distinguish between a vividly imagined experience and an actual one.*" When you imagine your dream outcome, your brain prepares it and sends you subconscious instructions that lead you to manifest it. While you go through the struggles, keep that picture vivid and unshaken. It is where your dreams take on a form.

1.5 STOKING THE FLAMES: DAILY HABITS TO KEEP YOUR FIRE ALIVE

The reality is that *motivation does not stay with you permanently after you first receive it.*" The flame requires daily maintenance for it to stay alive. The finding of motivation does not automatically sustain it. You have to nurture it. Regular care allows the Fire to remain lit because neglecting it will cause the flame to extinguish. Achieving your goals does not require massive, challenging assignments. The essential thing is to appear present each day. Your initial goal excitement may fade quickly during the first stages of goal pursuit and sustaining it beyond this phase is highly challenging. However, if you can drive it forward without failure, you can achieve your goals. "*Daily habits create momentum*." Your alignment with goals remains strong when you dedicate daily time slots for work, keep gratitude notes, and check vision checkpoints.

Reflection represents one of the most vigorous habits that individuals should develop. "*You should dedicate time daily to measure your advancement and make methodical adjustments.*" Asking yourself a few straightforward questions at the end of the day is a good idea. "*What went well today, and what could I improve for tomorrow?*" This behavior continuously supports your goals and keeps you moving in the right direction. Reflection requires more than just observing past events, as it also involves creating plans. "*People who succeed the most never respond to what life presents them; they proactively shape it.*"

The key component for keeping the Fire alive is expressed through gratitude. "*Your goals remain steadfast through the strength that gratitude provides*." Gratitude shifts your awareness by focusing on your past achievements rather than unfulfilled desires. Checking your accomplishments whenever possible will keep your energy burning bright and stop you from becoming exhausted. Paying attention to your commitment after dealing with a problematic assignment sets a good example of goal stoking. "*A victory exists in every positive movement toward your goals; therefore, find reasons to rejoice at every small achievement.*"

Daily consistency is the most essential habit that will lead you towards success. "*A major factor that sets success from failure emerges through consistent actions*." The flame of motivation may temporarily vanish, but continuous movement sustains your drive. Set yourself up to perform something that advances your goal achievement on every challenging day, regardless of your incremental progress. Your attitude remains favorable toward your momentum because you continue acting daily despite your doubts. Motivation does not mean you are always excited about each task because motivated people do tasks even when they do not feel excited. You must take the required actions regardless of your feelings about the task. The persistent maintenance of your Fire will grow more intense as time goes on; thus, you must maintain constant vigilance to prevent it from burning out.

Your daily habits function as the leading force for achieving lasting success. "*The fundamental elements of achieving significant goals consist of repeated small actions.*" Your consistent repetition of these habits will eventually produce big-scale achievements. Daily feeding of your Fire will lead you toward achieving your dreams.

CHAPTER 2

THE ANVIL OF SELF IS YOUR CORE

INTRODUCTION

Building self-confidence starts like a great blacksmith's work, which is meticulously shaped and polished by extreme heat and pressure. Every challenge presents an opportunity to shape belief by hitting the iron. People forge their confidence through all decisions while actively thinking about and acting during challenging moments, much like the blacksmith hammers iron in the forge. First, confidence feels fragile. When unhelpful thoughts about your inadequacy appear to you, it becomes simple to question your abilities. The concern about failure creates such strong paralysis that taking the next step becomes impossible. "*The decisive decision now rests between surrender and a determined response.*" The right choice is to fight, to recognize that the voice of doubt is simply a challenge waiting to be overcome. Confidence grows through each bold action taken against those fears. Replacing "*I can't*" with "*I will*" becomes the first significant strike, laying the foundation for stronger self-belief.

Every obstacle a person encounters leads to a bigger opportunity, just as the blacksmith is aware that each hammer blow takes the metal closer to its intended use. Similar to that process, "*Failure brings resilience to those who use it as a tool to build strength.*" A person is not defined by their failures.

Every setback becomes a crucial component in shaping one's identity. The critical truth emerges: the path ends at failure only because success stems from this point. The strength of determination grows with each challenging situation, regardless of the intensity of the agony. The real capabilities of consistency emerge when we put in our daily tasks with a determined focus. Through unceasing hammering, the blacksmith obtains progressively better precision while reinforcing the strength of their completed work. A person develops self-confidence by enduring continuous, steady effort. "*Belief develops into a reality through repetitive daily work combined with displaying stability.*"

Perceived slowness should not prevent individuals from developing confidence with each hammer strike; the metal transforms from weak to stronger and takes on meaningful shapes, representing continuous life action. Daily commitments form the foundation of dependable confidence as people develop their belief systems through proven actions. The journey of confidence leads from the external world into a deeper, internal fortification that cannot be easily shaken. "*Confidence determines itself by its resistance towards challenges rather than external opinions because inner beliefs create the measure of personal strength.*" This transformation comes through years of confronting fears, battling doubts, and guarding the sense of purpose that guides you forward.

The more consistently you invest in this daily grind of self-empowerment, the more solid the base becomes until confidence rests on something unshakable. Like a blacksmith's refined blade, the final masterpiece reflects true confidence. Possessing absolute confidence means carrying oneself with dignity in the face of challenges, even when mistakes occur. It is not perfection but resilience to face life's challenges with an unwavering belief in oneself that makes confidence true and lasting.

2.1 THE ANVIL PRINCIPLE: WHY CHALLENGES BUILD STRENGTH

Nobody's life has been a straight line; everyone experiences ups and downs, flips, and failures, and we all try to live with them. Every individual is different, and they all try to break free from some unseen bonds. Only those without limitations truly exist. Just as the day has no boundaries, neither does the night, which reveals the beauty of the stars and the moon. "*When we strive to overcome our constraints, it becomes easier to navigate through crises.*" Such thoughts can help those in distress survive and endure.

We should aspire to soar, not just beneath the sky above, but also within the depths of our strong minds. *When the sky calls, how can our wings remain unspread?* We ought to live with the dreams of the sky, even when clouds darken it. If you believe you can achieve your goals, they will remain within reach. Conversely, if you tell yourself, you can't, defeat will surely follow. Remember one thing: *Our beliefs shape our reality.*" Time may seem to fly, but when we take control of it, true success happens. Our real abilities emerge when we accomplish what we once thought was impossible.

People develop resilience and strength through the vital life challenges and troublesome obstacles they face. You stand at a blacksmith's forge while they expose an unformed metal object to hot flames in the fire. When struck by hammers, the metal develops from its weak state into stronger forms with meaningful designs. "*The metal transformation through this process shares the same objective as human development throughout our lives*." Painful situations strike us like blacksmith hammers, producing inner strength similar to that of iron forging. "*Every obstacle attacks our inherent weakness during the transformation process, thus contributing to our development of an infallible structure*." Blacksmiths employ heat-based metal processing techniques to manufacture powerful metal forms; similarly, people evolve in challenging life scenarios. "*Life brings difficulties to which we should react as mechanisms that sculpt our personality*."

The most effective growth occurs when challenges coexist with setbacks and impediments. The power of a hammer striking iron surfaces presents a tremendous challenge, causing people to face their limitations as they suffer pain and develop their abilities. Through transformational processes, people can achieve greater goals by transforming untapped potential resources into powerful components. Life challenges function similarly to forge fires, transforming our abilities to overcome life's obstacles. "*Pressure and difficulties develop into robust, confident results by transforming weaknesses and uncertainties.*"

Life experiences transform survivors into wiser and more confident people who remain transformed beyond their prior condition. Metal needs heat exposure to be forged; similarly, confidence is shaped in challenges and uncertainties. The defining aspect that creates confidence is adversity. The process of facing difficulties turns uncertain beliefs into the most potent form of self-assurance. "*Each obstacle creates a strong impact that tests character development by building determination within the person.*" The challenges that you face will build your character, as they cannot eliminate your presence. Mastering various obstacles builds your competence level, and it eventually gives you absolute confidence about your ability to manage every situation.

From the moment we are born, all humans understand the natural process of treating hardships as destructive forces that they aim to escape from. "*Challenging circumstances lead to hidden prospects which eliminate the need to label them as enemies*." Life challenges present opportunities for you to deepen your dedication and uncover hidden strengths within yourself. "*Your capacity to perceive strength objectively forms through facing obstacles instead of evading them.*" Tests create true resilience, whereas ease creates no resilience. "*Confrontation of challenges creates unbreakable inner confidence by experiencing how life tests you.*"

A challenge stands out from other difficult circumstances in our approach to dealing with them. Dealing with obstacles leads people to permanent self-development when they learn new capabilities through disciplinary training gained from challenges. "*Our ability to gain power while learning valuable skills for future challenges develops as we face and overcome every demanding hurdle.*" When individuals resist adversity, they get permanently changed because they gain fresh perceptions about themselves with a deeper understanding of the world around them.

Survivors of adversity develop new capabilities to face future challenges after successfully overcoming these experiences. Life adversity instills permanent strength that remains unaffected by others. "*People develop enduring, strong self-confidence through every challenge they overcome.*" Experiencing resilience naturally creates automatic confidence in people. The anvil principle offers a basic yet fundamental teaching that requires people to maintain the adversities they encounter before creating personal strength during challenging moments. Embracing adversity during personal growth enables people to gain greater confidence along with acquired skills that make them future ready.

2.2 THE CONFIDENCE FORGE: REFRAMING FAILURE AS GROWTH FAILURES ARE UNAVOIDABLE IN OUR LIVES

It might appear when one least expects it and tests one's resolve in several ways throughout life. Failure is a component of success rather than its Imagine a blacksmith standing in front of his workshop's anvil, holding a hammer. With each hammer strike, he transforms raw metal into a powerful, practical tool. Failure functions similarly. It shapes and molds a person's character with every challenge faced. Converting failure into growth has proven to be the most useful path for developing confidence.

The blacksmith refuses to end his strikes after delivering the initial blow. While melting occurs, the metal becomes stronger and more resilient through repetitive hitting during heat exposure. Similarly, people should respond to failure by refusing to surrender. Failure is a crucial process contributing to personal growth; therefore, people must view it as part of the development path. People who acknowledge failure for what it is will understand that it unlocks personal growth without blocking their path to achievement.

The blacksmith continues to heat the metal after his first strike in the forge. Multiple hammering processes and shaping procedures transform the object into something stronger, increasing its value. Failure serves as a teaching mechanism, allowing people to acquire knowledge and ultimately achieve better results. "*Discovery of failure as an inevitable component of progress leads people to build stronger confidence in themselves.*" Every struggle provides valuable learning material that enables people to improve their performance, simultaneously with their problem-solving skills and mental strength. People who embrace failure will build stronger confidence and self-assurance.

To establish a lasting sense of self-belief, a person must adopt a different perspective. "*Every failure provides value because it enables people to develop new skills as they improve their techniques*." Outstanding accomplishments often emerge from learning experiences that result from multiple failures, ultimately leading individuals toward their ultimate achievements. Confrontation with failure while learning effective strategies increases resilience and confidence. The learning experience through failure develops inner confidence, proving that failure is a natural part of human growth rather than a source of fear.

The blacksmith understands that the initial blow marks commencement. To forge stronger metal pieces through a series of successive hammer hits, one must be patient and persistent. In a similar vein, building confidence calls for consistent work, learning from mistakes, and being receptive to new concepts. People grow more capable and more determined because of each setback, which gives them unflinching faith in their future successes. "*Confidence is not born from avoiding failure, but from facing it head-on, learning from each experience, and continuing the journey forward*."

Elon Musk suffered numerous devastating setbacks before achieving success in the tech world. His early SpaceX rockets exploded, and Tesla teetered on the edge of bankruptcy. Instead of crumbling, each failure fueled him; defeats were not setbacks but data to refine and improve. Each one became a steppingstone, and the setbacks became part of the creation of greater resilience and innovation. The same goes for Michael Jordan, who was probably the greatest basketball player of all time, and was cut by his high school team. Instead of giving up, he put in more work and used reversal to run faster. That is why these stories show you do not need to be constantly successful to build your confidence; it is grown through failure.

If we change how we view failure, we can turn stumbling blocks into steppingstones as we build a conversation with ourselves about how great we are and with every fall and rise. Accepting failure gives people the confidence to take risks without worrying about being rejected. Failure no longer can immobilize individuals; rather, it serves as a tool for progress. When failure is seen as a normal part of the process, it no longer has the power to obstruct progress. Every lesson learned from failure serves as a source of inspiration to improve abilities and self-worth. To conclude, "*Failure is your strongest partner, guiding you towards self-assurance and success*."

2.3 THE MIRROR OF SELF-ESTEEM: SEEING YOUR TRUE VALUE

Recognizing that your value doesn't come from external validation, achievements, or appearance but from the inherent worth you carry simply by being yourself. A confident base develops from our firm internal belief, which surpasses external commendations and momentary successes. Looking at your reflection while facing the mirror would provide the experience. Reflections that display doubt, insecurity, and dependence on others' approval signal unstable confidence in the mirror. You must cultivate this confidence by understanding your inherent worth.

The foundation of developing genuine confidence begins within, much like a craftsman's work through their artful creations. Your self-esteem influences both your interactions with others and how others perceive you. Those with weak self-esteem often feel empty, regardless of how much external success or public acclaim they achieve. "*Such unstable confidence bases cannot maintain their strength because approval and failure constantly shape their stability.*" A person's self-esteem is an inner foundation that stands as an unchanging force, sustaining true and enduring confidence. People watch themselves in mirrors but interpret different images in various ways. "*Your face represents just an external part of your essential nature.*"

A self-valuing person observes their entire nature, including their abilities, and accepts their incomplete aspects simultaneously. When you observe your reflection in the mirror, it shows your deep-rooted belief in your value because others' assessments do not shape your self-image. *Core beliefs define the value of self rather than observations from external sources.*" Internal conviction about your worth does not depend on external world opinions.

Most individuals initiate their quest for confidence by seeking validation from external sources. People who experience low self-esteem constantly seek validation from others due to a sense of inner emptiness that fuels their need for external approval. The genuine satisfaction that acceptance should offer remains incomplete because real completion only comes from accepting oneself. Your self-confidence develops from accepting your entire being, including every fault.

Self-awareness enables you to avoid external approvals as your confidence becomes impervious to challenge. Once you know your value, you stop searching for validation since you already possess self-awareness of your worth. Lasting self-assurance is built on this kind of understanding. Self-esteem stands independent of your perfect character. Your path to success involves recognizing your deserving nature, which stands beyond perfection to achieve happiness and fulfillment. Your perspective begins to change after you realize your value. Your confidence grows independently of your perfection because you understand that you already embody enough worth through your current state.

The practice of recalling your core values and natural worth strengthens the base of your confidence. By understanding your true value, you can stay steady when faced with criticism or challenges. *Your self-esteem enables a form of confidence that no external threat can break."* Understanding your value enables you to disempower hurtful external criticism and handle dissatisfying encounters.

Your realization of personal value makes it impossible for others to damage your inner conviction. Your worth manifests itself through your conduct instead of your feelings alone. Your path to your objectives will carry purpose, strength, and power as you face difficult situations with courage. Your authentic self-reveals its true power by projecting confidence outwards toward the world. Building an unbreakable inner confidence enables you to advance through life with integrity.

2.4 THE BLUEPRINT OF BELIEF: DESIGNING YOUR CONFIDENCE ROUTINE

Confidence emerges through deliberate steps rather than accidental occurrences, as it requires purposeful and patient construction. A professional architect would start with building plans as their first step before construction. Organizations must develop a blueprint to define the entire construction process, from start to finish, before commencing the building project. Similarly, *'A blueprint helps an individual to build strong structures as confidence needs a strategic framework to become established*." This blueprint encompasses more than just ideas, as it combines meaningful actions and habitual thoughts that foster self-belief over time.

Constructing a resilient mindset follows the same deliberate approach as blueprint development. One builds confidence by keeping up continuous work without interruption. When establishing self-confidence, individuals need to follow a step-by-step approach, much like constructing a building. A person's ability to create confidence largely depends on their ability to maintain consistency. "*The process takes time because steady, purposeful practices drive the development*." Every incremental development, no matter how small, leads to a more substantial foundation of self-belief over an extended period.

As you engage in daily positive thinking and goal-oriented work while reviewing your progress, your identity evolves into that of a confident person. A first appearance shows four basic components of this routine: affirmation and goal setting, physical activity, and mental reflection. The daily practices you conduct transform into an automatic mindset of belief that resides within your mind. Each action acts as a single brick, contributing to your confidence foundation because architects focus on precise brick placements. Consistent practice of these methods produces confidence that eventually becomes a natural aspect of your identity. Building belief requires more than positive thinking alone, as it necessitates specific, meaningful actions to develop. The power of belief needs active pursuit to move ahead.

All attempts, regardless of their scale, work to expand the belief. Each positive action you take, regardless of size, helps you believe success remains attainable to you. "*Every action you undertake, regardless of its apparent triviality, guides you toward adopting beliefs that success is attainable*." Tiny accomplishments from day to day build into substantial progress, which builds confidence persistently every day. Putting additional effort into this routine will strengthen confidence, which provides better protection against life's inevitable obstacles.

Self-reflection represents the final essential component in the arrangement of confidence-building principles. After architects evaluate their work, they ensure that everything remains true to their initial design plan; similarly, you need to evaluate your progress regularly as well. "*Connecting self-observation helps track progress areas, supplying developmental methods and acceptance of accomplished achievements*." Your mind achieves better concentration and remains on track with its principal objective by performing periodic goal assessments and progress reviews.

Regularly checking your current situation is an essential factor in maintaining and strengthening your confidence. The blueprint sets you on a path that will create an extraordinary change in your mindset. Over time, your routine will become second nature. The establishment of belief structures leads to an increase in self-confidence over time. Thus, the systematic implementation of your plan progressively develops confidence until it becomes an integral part of your personality.

Your self-confidence evolves from being an objective target, which becomes your fundamental identity. The blueprint you follow changes how you perform while impacting what you think and transforming your attitude to adopt a successful mindset.

2.5 THE UNSHAKABLE CORE: STAYING GROUNDED IN YOUR TRUTH

In this world, you get pulled in different directions. It could be due to expectations, comparisons, failures, or criticisms, among other factors. In such dynamic environments, we should be able to build proper inner foundations based on certain values and beliefs, so that no storm can shake us. True confidence comes from being deeply honest with yourself. Solid ground remains steady under your feet when you stand up on it while all the storms rage around you. Authentic foundations of confidence resist any attempts at being shaken. Your authentic self serves as your firm foundation because it exists too deeply to be shaken by opposition or criticism.

Your genuine confidence grows through personal awareness rather than relying on positive opinions from others. Trust in yourself bolsters your confidence to new levels of strength. Core values build your confidence into an unbreakable fortress that remains protected from outside criticism and assessment. Challenges do not easily influence people who have built their identity based on what is true within them. Their foundation ensures permanent stability because external changes and disagreements neither affect nor shift them. Their inner stability enables them to maintain their position during external world transformations.

Having a constant center enables you to develop confidence that lasts through time. Unraveling your confidence requires answering a fundamental inquiry about your identity: "*Who am I*?" Your authentic self-reveals when you grasp what you truly believe in, along with your essential values and the purpose behind your existence. Self-awareness builds a solid base in the same way as a constructor who pours stable concrete before starting to construct high towers. "*Establishing truth enables strong, unbreakable confidence because you act according to your beliefs.*"

Living in alignment with your core values allows you to develop indestructible confidence, which remains strong and resilient. The loss of basic principles or compromise of essential beliefs will lead to a serious weakening of your foundation. Letting go of fundamental values reduces personal confidence in a person's life. Your authentic life, free from fakeness, promotes stability in your confidence because you stay true to yourself. Your foundation of authenticity will protect your stability, but more importantly, it creates an opportunity to flourish. With such certainty that your identity suffices as-is, you can conquer every test that stands in your way.

Deciding to build your beliefs upon truth enables you to resist life challenges through unyielding determination. Their unshakable self-assurance is matched by unwavering focus, driven by the understanding that their true self is their greatest asset. With inner strength, confidence remains unaffected by difficult circumstances. They recognize that an individual's identity exists solely because of what they know to be true within themselves. The foundation of authenticity develops into lasting confidence because it provides unshakable stability. Authenticity as a foundation creates adaptability, which allows your confidence to survive whatever stands in your way. True self-precision enables people to address life challenges with unwavering determination.

CHAPTER 3

THE HAMMER OF DISCIPLINE – CRAFTING CONSISTENCY

INTRODUCTION

Inside the small, dim forge, the rhythmic strikes of a hammer upon an anvil produce echoing sounds through the air. The blacksmith uses purposeful blows to create attractive, functional pieces from raw metal. The blacksmith proceeds with patience as he understands that different strikes will ultimately define the metal's final structure. The disciplined hammer creates equal results to those achieved by the blacksmith as he molds metal through his work. Discipline is the hammer that creates excellence. It is a precise tool that is persistent, unflinching, and transformational. It transforms intention into action and dreams into reality with every blow, transforming undeveloped potential into refined skill. Progress is steadily fueled by discipline. Procrastination, sloth, and long-lasting habits are all broken by the hammer of discipline.

Before undertaking any strike, the blacksmith requires a specific plan; similarly, a person must create a plan for success. Real progress requires proper planning since an undefined plan prevents actual development. A blueprint emerges from consistent daily activities of thoughts and actions, which create the fundamentals of long-lasting success and confidence. "*The steady dedication and continuous efforts resulting from routine activities produce final results.*" The creation of discipline requires defined purposes because it develops through a process of planning and implementation.

People should adopt the attitude of blacksmiths who value consistent practices. People easily lose focus due to temporary highs, lows, and short-lived bursts of energy. The blacksmith understands that all small blows contribute to the completion of their work. Every tiny advancement and minimal contribution accumulate to form vital progression throughout life.

Growth occurs when one maintains discipline through one's actions. Time works as the necessary period and the means to create durable outcomes. Achieving success emerges from building it through continuous, planned, and deliberate actions without relying on a premature significant achievement. "*The blacksmith molds metals through each of his blows, similarly to how disciplined action forms individual life trajectories*." Discipline is a tool that enables slow but purposeful progress toward success by consistently ordering actions.

3.1 THE HAMMER TECHNIQUE: BREAKING GOALS INTO ACTIONABLE STRIKES

The blacksmith labors in front of his anvil, where the heated metal glows with red warmth. He has already created a strategic plan at the beginning of each blow. He avoids shaping the entire metal in one stage because he realizes the metal requires gradual progress until its final form emerges. "*Through the hammer technique, people can divide their goals into attainable steps*." This process transforms overwhelming targets into specific and producible steps.

Individuals who want to achieve their larger goals need to break them down into smaller steps that are easier to accomplish, much like a blacksmith operates. "*Each minor assignment leads an individual closer to reaching their most significant objective.*" When people focus on individual assignments, the massive size of their primary objective is reduced to workable dimensions. "*Through small daily actions, a person creates an increasing momentum that drives them toward their goals."* Success requires walking through life by strategically taking one small step at a time.

When using the hammer technique, users can create precise tasks. True success emerges from tackling one small task at a time rather than trying to handle everything concurrently. The blacksmith avoids attempting to change the entire metal object through a single blow. His goal with every strike is exactness, leading to an optimized performance in his actions. Success is achieved when you avoid rushing and concentrate on completing each step one at a time.

When people transform their massive goals into smaller, manageable ones, the pathway toward success becomes clearer. Dividing the journey into smaller sections produces less fear and makes goals simpler to reach. Every separate movement you make in the right direction contributes to an accumulating progressive journey. Each strike of the hammer and each movement leaves you one step closer to reaching your final objective, according to the hammer technique.

The method of steady progress and the time spent moving forward equals the value of achieving your dream, so consistent pursuit becomes necessary for success. When applied to complex tasks, the hammer technique enables individuals to transform unachievable goals into achievable realities. "*Your path toward success becomes manageable through focusing on solitary steps that lead to ultimate achievement*." Any completed small task leads you steadily toward your vision. Each of us can improve ourselves by striking our goals with the same focus and effort as a blacksmith hitting metal.

3.2 THE RHYTHM OF REPETITION: WHY CONSISTENCY BEATS INTENSITY

The blacksmith bangs metal with a well-timed percussion within the workshop's silence. The rhythm exists because of continuous effort rather than the intensity of the blow. Through repetition, one establishes a work of art without depending on powerful individual strikes. *"Intense bursts of effort alone will not create success since consistency becomes crucial for reaching success*."

Continuous drumming by hammer strokes of the blacksmith produces actual achievements in the workshop.

Building success demands continuous and regular movements rather than brief spurts of energetic actions." People often lose themselves in dreams about pushing the limits of their efforts, as they believe that concentrated effort can lead to achievement. Through repetitive actions, the blacksmith comes to understand that success emerges from disciplined practice. Constant, unbroken rhythmic effort maintains true power as the fundamental source of achievement.

For enduring success, one must maintain consistent behavior. "*The instant positive outcomes from intense effort become permanent when people apply consistent behavior.*" Multiple repetitive blows from the blacksmith hammer create a greater unified achievement than a single forceful hit could accomplish. Multiple strikes add momentum to each other until they form a stronger, more resilient result. Small actions performed consistently everyday result in the gradual development of long-term success in life and any other venture.

People often expect instant results. Success develops through continuous and prolonged dedicated work rather than appearing instantly. Success requires patience and persistence, which repetition teaches through rhythmic learning. Extended consistent action development enables individuals to build enough momentum, which drives them toward enduring achievement. A determined and controlled approach through time leads you toward your objectives rather than impulsive, sudden actions. The blacksmith achieves success through constant repetition. "*The blacksmith achieves beautiful, strong results through his continuous, purposeful process*." People who recognize consistent action as the foundation for success will develop long-lasting achievements through their repetitive behaviors.

3.3 THE DISCIPLINE FORGE: BUILDING HABITS THAT LAST

In the heart of the blacksmith's workshop, the forge burns bright with heat. For the blacksmith to make enduring objects, he must first construct a reliable base. Maintaining discipline in the discipline forge means that people establish consistent activities that are the basis for their success. To forge lasting habits, you need the same three elements that metal needs in the forge: *dedicated time, coupled with work, and continuous adherence to the process*.

The metal formation process at the forge produces items that acquire strength and longevity. Regular use of disciplined behavior leads to the development of success. The structure of lasting success relies on habits, as they serve as its foundational framework. The process of metal-shaping demands repeated cycles of heating and hammering from the blacksmith, just like individuals need to maintain disciplined habits for future transformation.

Building lasting habits requires focus. The blacksmith focuses on the metal; people must concentrate on their daily deeds to generate enduring changes. Just as the forge operation continues beyond one blow, individuals in their daily endeavors should adopt the same approach. A person achieves their future through ongoing, regular actions. Achieving enduring success requires the time-based performance of purposeful, small actions that accumulate to advance greater professional goals.

The development of habits depends on maintaining steady conduct. Repeating the same action helps routine integration, generating enduring positive modifications. The step-by-step application of disciplined habits leads to the same outcome as shaping metal within a forge. Success endures because of the power of habits. "*Your goals are fulfilled through developing habits that construct an organized system that drives you to your desired results.*" So we should create successful habits, much like a blacksmith creates tools for a reason.

3.4 THE POWER OF SMALL WINS: CELEBRATING PROGRESS ALONG THE WAY

The blacksmith does not wait for the thing to be almost finished before celebrating. Each small victory, the first strike of the hammer, the first successful shaping of the metal, is a cause for celebration. Reaching little goals will help you stay motivated and maintain your vacation schedule, giving you constant inspiration and momentum. Living the long path of life becomes overwhelming, yet a simple solution exists to maintain focus through victory celebrations.

Each small win builds momentum. "*Your program of celebrating small successes develops a belief that you can reach your intended, most significant targets*." Although these minor achievements hold little weight in the overall success framework, they are the key building blocks that power genuine triumphs. People achieve better self-confidence as they recognize their small achievements while continuing to advance. "*Small successes*' effectiveness lies in their ability to maintain your driving force toward significant targets.

Throughout the process, the blacksmith marks every success with the awareness that steady progression leads him toward completing his work. "*The impact of each hammer blow adds up to the primary purpose while functioning as an individual win.*" Individuals should acknowledge every minor achievement that occurs while pursuing their targets. "*Progressive increases throughout the travel provide the necessary energy to keep pushing ahead.*"

Small achievements indicate that progress is being made. You will see a successful approach when you focus on your accomplishments. Celebrating small achievements helps people sustain their motivation and maintain optimism. Personal triumphs strengthen the belief that success is possible and provide the inner fortitude required to aim for even higher goals.

Before being widely admired, Stephen King, the famous American author, received piles of rejection letters and hung them on a nail in his house. And all of those letters, positive or negative, demonstrated to him that he was making progress and trying to become better. King's triumph with the novel *Carrie* was the result of numerous small victories spacing out over time rather than a single noteworthy accomplishment. In a similar vein, Simone Biles, the greatest American gymnast, did not become famous suddenly. Building her career and talents step by step enabled her to become a legend. Examining their examples, we see that the climb to greatness tends to be a gradual process. It's made up of many intentional little decisions. Small achievements maintain our motivation, make us believe in ourselves, and prove that respecting even the most minor improvements is essential.

The development of substantial achievements starts with achieving regular minor victories. You will develop momentum and confidence when you are clear about your direction and by celebrating your minor successes. The blacksmith understands that every minor achievement moves him progressively nearer to his objective; thus, People need to follow this same approach. Success achieves inevitability when people identify and celebrate their minor accomplishments.

3.5 THE MASTER'S STRIKE: STAYING FOCUSED

When motivation fades despite the cooling forge, the blacksmith maintains his position. His method of success relies on his training and skill, coupled with his discipline, rather than short-lived bursts of motivation. A person who possesses the master's strike maintains concentration without motivation when they resolve weaknesses. "*Progress through life depends on discipline rather than motivation, and this tends to disappear.*"

What the master knows is that the work must continue, regardless of fading motivation. The master continues with purpose after motivational excitement ends because discipline serves as his driving force, not motivation. People must maintain their dedication toward their goals even though motivation begins to fade. Success comes from consistent work regardless of whether motivation returns.

Discipline is what sustains progress. "*Discipline is the primary force that pushes work forward since it operates step by step after inspiration dies down.*" During the master's strike, the main priority remains consistency since members must consistently appear, execute their assignments, and maintain their commitment to the primary goal. The real key to success lies in persistence and discipline, more than simply performing with intense effort. The master identifies the true beginning of work after motivation wanes. "*Masterful talent demonstrates its peak by retaining concentration even though motivation levels decline.*" Those who maintain their efforts continuously, without paying attention to their current feelings, will build sustained achievements.

CHAPTER 4

The Quench of Resilience – Tempering Your Spirit

INTRODUCTION

The blacksmith dips the glowing metal into a bucket of water, filling the air with the intense hiss of steam as the metal rapidly cools, hardens, and solidifies. Quench refers to the process that makes the metal durable and resilient. Like a blacksmith's work, resilience is made through fire and trials. When people are put in the deep end, they achieve far more than they think. The hammer and quench are a necessary step to each other: every challenge faced will empower your inner strength, even if it is shaped like a tough piece of metal.

The hardest trials may feel like they could break us, but when we face them with courage, it becomes the fire that tempers our spirit into an unshakeable strength. "*Resilience is not a result of denial, the denial of adversity; it's the result of adversity.*" Mitigating and overcoming it will make us truly resilient. As it does to the blacksmith, the blacksmith's careful quenching process can harden the metal. Just as this process can make the blacksmith tougher, it can also make us more resilient and better able to cope with the world.

Resilience built in the heat of adversity becomes the strength to lay the foundation to face future challenges. The repeated trials, repeated hammer strikes of adversity, build up the unyielding core of who we are. The quenching is not a quick process; it requires patience, akin to the slow-burning forge, and precision, akin to a blacksmith's measured hand strikes. There are no shortcuts for resilience, only a steady hammer that promptly shapes you into an unbreakable person. Every failure and every difficult situation are a part of the forging process, a tempering of the spirit that is unbreakable. At every setback, we will become stronger, learning to manage any situation.

Every effort, no matter how tiny, is an act of rebellion against stagnation on the growth path. Trying is rejecting the falsehood that denial whispers that standing motionless is strength, and that hesitating is safety. Indecision masquerades as patience, but real development necessitates having the guts to act, even when the step seems inconsequential. "*Being resilient is the ability to climb out of the ashes of defeat more fierce, sharp, and determined*." Hardships also prepare us to handle greater challenges in the future, just as the quenching of a piece of metal results in a product that can withstand greater pressure and force. Indeed, we survive in the heat of adversity, but we also thrive and surpass what we were before.

Let us never forget that our resilience, like the blacksmith's work, is a task for time. We grow a spirit that cannot be broken by constant effort and overcoming difficulties. When our spirit is quenched, we become weak and lose our strength, courage, and unwavering determination. Each trial makes us more capable of turning difficulty into an advantage.

4.1 THE QUENCH EFFECT: HOW SETBACKS MAKE YOU STRONGER

The forge glows brightly as the metal burns within. Blacksmith strikes it repeatedly, forming and fomenting it for a different purpose. With each blow, the blacksmith's hammer shapes unyielding metal in an unrelenting rhythm. A trial by fire and ice, the flaming steel withstands the blows and bends to the craftsman's desire before being thrown into the cooling water. Despite appearing as a harsh jolt, failures like the quenching bath soften the soul and replace brittleness with fortitude. There would be no power without fire, no edge without the hammer, and no true mettle without the dive into icy uncertainty. "*The quenching effect reveals the true strength of the metal; similarly, the setbacks show the true strength in us*."

In life, setbacks are often viewed as moments of weakness or defeat, but they can also be times of growth. ‘‘*Setbacks are not obstacles to success; they're the retort for realization.*’’ Failures, each one, make us more complicated and stronger so that we can endure whatever stands before us. The quenching effect is not instantaneous; rather, it is a necessary one. Just as the metal must be quenched repeatedly to achieve its final form unyieldingly, in the same way, resilience is achieved through time and repeated challenges. "*The lack of challenges does not build true strength; true strength is built in the face of challenges with the ability to overcome them and become stronger each time*." That is why the blacksmith knows risks can be involved in quenching. Just as we do with setbacks, we must handle the challenges carefully. "*In each challenge, we get more resilient by getting used to the pressure and not breaking down under it.*" The setbacks that come our way in life are not meant to destroy us but to make us stronger, to be forged, and to become different things, becoming more inclined as time passes.

Abraham Lincoln could have ended his political career after the presidential election did not go his way. Instead, that experience helped toughen his will and improve his leadership skills. In the years that followed, he would help a divided nation navigate its most challenging times. In the same way, Lady Gaga (a Famous American Singer) lost her first label only months after signing; however, that only encouraged her and made her more passionate about music. Once she returned, her ambition was clear and forceful, and her vision changed pop culture. These stories demonstrate the quench effect. Difficulties are not your end, but they allow you to grow, form, and strengthen. Not giving up after facing failure means you return stronger, smarter, and more determined.

We learn from the quenching that setbacks aren't the end; they're the start of another strength level. Just as the quenching water hardens the metal, our spirit is hardened by the things we overcome. Many setbacks remind us that we can persevere and continue on our journey to achieve our goals. In that process, we become unbreakable.

4.2 THE RESILIENCE RITUAL: BOUNCING BACK WITH GRACE

In the silence of the forge, the blacksmith strikes the hammer with the same intent and care each time. After every stroke, he examines the metal for any weakness and then applies his precision with firmness and painstaking care. A ritual of unrelenting labor and meticulous accuracy is necessary for the blacksmith's art to forge not only metal but also unbreakable toughness. Every blow and movement is intentional. The same qualities are required for mastery in each art form; *perseverance, repetition, and a steadfast dedication to the flame that tempers excellence*. Bouncing back with grace is not simply surviving setbacks; that's not enough. True resilience is the ability to bounce back, learn from every failure, and use it as a steppingstone to become stronger.

The resilience ritual entails persevering through challenges with unwavering determination and flexibility. It will be that which makes us strong, able to rise after every setback, bend but never break, and transform life's most devastating blows into opportunities for growth. "*To become resilient, one must accept the recovery rituals, knowing how to get up and do something of purpose even when you fall.*" As the blacksmith strikes the metal back and forth, he is brought closer to his finished product. Every step in overcoming a challenge fortifies us, making us a bit stronger. Every challenge faced fortifies us a bit more.

The blacksmith turns imperfections in the metal to their advantage, working with the metal until it is perfect. Just like that, we must learn to approach challenges with the same mindset, treating setbacks as opportunities to grow stronger rather than failures. *"Resilience is a process of continual attempts to learn how to persevere through life's hardship with integrity and courage.*" Whenever we overcome a challenge, there is another layer to our resilience. The point of this process is not about achieving perfection but about getting better, learning, and improving.

The resilience ritual means facing every setback gracefully and knowing that they will all bring us closer to our ultimate destination. We repeatedly go through the resilience ritual, learning to overcome challenges with quiet strength, recovering from the fall, and returning with unbelievable determination. We must work resolutely against life's apathy, creating meaning via unrelenting effort, just like the blacksmith who converts the raw metal into a form by hammering with patience and persistence.

4.3 THE HEAT OF ADVERSITY: EMBRACING CHALLENGES AS OPPORTUNITIES

As the blacksmith bends the metal into respectable pieces of art, the flames licking at it heat the metal, softening it in the forge. "*What goes in the furnace becomes purified through the heat of adversity.*" Although challenges and difficulties are frequently seen as barriers to growth, they serve as growth accelerators, inspiring us to take risks and push ourselves beyond our comfort zones.

As with metal, which must be heated to reach its peak performance, we must harden ourselves to the fires of life to discover our best. The blacksmith knows that the black metal must be heated to an intense temperature to become strong. "*Adversity is melodiously heated, and that heat transforms us as it transforms the metal into the forge.*" The battles are where our actual potential is shown; they must test us, drive us to the edge, and reveal new strengths and solutions within us. Although it is a complex process, growth requires it.

By viewing obstacles as chances, we can use widespread hardship as a driving force for transformation. Every difficult moment is an opportunity to learn, adapt, and grow stronger until it is time to move on to the next phase of our journey. "*We become stronger than before in the heat of our adversity, our capacity to endure and overcome.*" It does not break the blacksmith's metal in the heat of the forge, nor break us, in the strength of adversity, into individuals who will not attain their highest goals.

The most influential people in history, like artists, leaders, and innovators, were not molded in comfort. They were honed by strife, tempered by adversity, and hammered by failure. A challenge is an opportunity to develop rather than a barrier to overcome. Rejection instills resolve. Wisdom is deepened by loss, and the limits of what we think we can handle are stretched by discomfort.

The willingness to stand amid the fire, rather than its intensity, is what separates those who fail from those who succeed. Instead of asking if we shall experience suffering, adversity asks *how shall we allow it to burn us to ashes, or will it transform us into something unbreakable?* Every failure is an opportunity to learn. Every setback is a disguised lesson. When life gets tough, keep in mind that it's your becoming, not your downfall. Enter the flames. Come out stronger.

4.4 THE RESILIENCE JOURNAL: TRACKING YOUR GROWTH THROUGH STRUGGLE

The most difficult times in life serve as milestones on the path to resilience rather than merely being barriers. More than just a chronicle of hardships, the Resilience Journal serves as a compass for your future, a map of your strengths, and an acknowledgement of your progress. The daily task of the blacksmith's workshop brings new problems and possibilities. The blacksmith keeps his records daily as he works, noting each stage, each adjustment, and each success. "*A resilience journal is a tool that enables us to capture our growth in our struggles*." This is what we document; our experiences, which allow us to gain insight into our progress and use failure to fuel further progress.

The resilience journal is a personal growth and transformation record. "*The journey of struggle helps us to know that we've gone through and are furthered.*" We will be able to recognize patterns in our behavior and our experience, which will make it easier and more confident for us to face a similar difficulty in the future. Every writing in the resilience diary serves as a reminder of the strength acquired from adversity. The blacksmith is working towards his final masterpiece, and with every step he takes, he is closer to achieving it. To track our progress, we should also recognize our small victories that lead to bigger accomplishments.

It is not just a record of setbacks; the resilience journal records the strength they developed. This gives us a new perception of our journey because each obstacle we face is a part of the building blocks to come. Our resilience journal, of course, reveals the evolution of our resilience just as the blacksmith's journal does of his work. "*With a resilience journal, we develop a roadmap for success, but one that also includes struggle as a key component.*" We should be aware of the value of our struggle because it helps us measure our growth through it.

By going through this process, an obstacle becomes an opportunity to grow, and our resilience allows us to achieve our ultimate goals. By putting difficulties in writing, emotions can be untangled, and storms can be transformed into tactics. Patterns emerge when earlier struggles are revisited; *Where did I bend? Where did I maintain my ground?* Recording failures turns them from scars into lessons learned.

4.5 THE TEMPERED SPIRIT: EMERGING UNBREAKABLE

The blacksmith is not done with his job until he has shaped, hardened, and tempered the metal. "*Tempered spirit is an adjective that describes someone who has emerged from the heat of adversity, a spirit unbreakable and resilient.*" Moreover, through the trials, we will be strengthened and tempered by life's challenges as we face them. Just as the blacksmith cares to make the metal with a precise process, we count ourselves among those who have come through the constant process of becoming unbreakable.

Tempering is a process of strength and refinement. "*We have to become unbreakable by going through the heat of adversity and coming out the other side with a spirit open to no shattering*." Every challenge brings us one step closer to a spirit that can survive anything life throws our way. This allows us to find our true strength, which is that we are unyielding and resilient. We shape our character as we work in the furnace of struggles, bending the solid and shaping it to our use or desire. However, the tempered spirit is not born easily; ease-born tempered spirits are tame and ludicrous. Our challenges are how we learn to learn the most about ourselves, giving us the strength we never knew we had.

The tempered spirit cannot be broken because it has been tempered in the fires of adversity and shaped by each trial and challenge faced. After we have gone through our struggles, when we get to the other side, we will be stronger, more resilient, and capable of achieving our goals. The blacksmith's work tells us that real strength comes only from discomfort and facing challenges with resolve. One tempered spirit will remain unbreakable. "*Perseverance and discipline are the keys that determine our endurance in the struggles of life*." Just like the blacksmith's metal coming out of the forge hardened and unyielding, so too do we rise from our struggles stronger and more than able to face any future challenges.

CHAPTER 5

THE FORGE OF PERSONALITY – DESIGNING YOUR UNIQUE IDENTITY

INTRODUCTION

Raw metal burns in a glowing forge and is formed by force and intention. A new hardened form emerges from this heat, and something formed by precision, defined by strength, emerges. Through trials, decisions, and reflection, the self becomes refined and can be trusted to speak frankly and be resilient. The path of identity starts from self-discovery, not imitation. The blacksmith does not copy another's design; instead, he follows the natural properties of the material before him. The basis of authenticity is a unique identity, and the discovery of one's natural form begins with accepting who they are. Heat in the forge brings out potential within the metal, just as challenges reveal the character traits that define them.

As it is, every decision made and each principle upheld shapes the mold of who we are. These factors work in a person as a blueprint, so that not only the behavior, but the intention, the direction, has something to rest on. These beliefs get ingrained in a person's personality through repeated behaviors. It takes time for this change to occur. As a result, it calls for our unwavering dedication to introspection and improvement. To stand out in a noisy world, boldness is insufficient. As forged tools are fashioned for a special use, personalities are formed for specific roles that no one can fill.

The forging of personality doesn't occur in isolation. Character is tested through connection, as metal is tested in the real world. The refined self attracts depth in others. Through sincere interaction, we gain insight into the whole dimension of identity. The lifetime of forging is a masterpiece, not a single moment. "*There is not just one version of us. Identity is a creation as long as we live a craft of fire, pressure, and choice into something unshakable.*" The journey through the forge conducts it from raw beginnings to refined individuality, from uniqueness to integrity, confidence in use, and purpose. It is not a copy but an original, strong, and ready to rewrite the world.

5.1 THE FORGE OF AUTHENTICITY: EMBRACING YOUR TRUE SELF

Authenticity is the greatest act of bravery in a world that wants to shape us into something easier to categorize. Living with authenticity means letting go of the masks we've put on to gain acceptance, safety, or survival—it doesn't mean striving for perfection. These masks vanish in the furnace of authenticity, leaving behind something unique and potent. A fresh, wet piece of metal catches the fire on the anvil in the corner of the blacksmith's shop. The blacksmith watches it; he must make something up and discover what it can be. "*Authenticity starts with observation, not invention, by honoring what already exists rather than creating something new.*"

The fire burns up the forge but does not determine the final shape. In addition to the shaping process, the core material is honored. Similarly. Since inner truth is the only location where true identity coincides, authentic behavior originates there rather than from borrowed expectations. The world frequently presents us with standards to meet, scripts to adhere to, and molds to suit. Authenticity, however, evolves rather than conforms. The objective is to improve the metal's inherent qualities rather than eliminate them, much like a blacksmith at a forge levels the hammer with purpose. The same is true of the self.

Being authentic means aligning yourself more deeply and intimately with your inner self rather than trying to become something completely different. The sparks that flare throughout this process are indicators of change rather than devastation. The constant hum of expectations in the world often prompts us to conform, to alter who we are to become more palatable and acceptable. Whispering voices Fit in, Gain favor. Avoid being conspicuous. Boundaries must be relaxed, identity must be traded for belonging, and acceptance must be traded for truth. But in the furnace of authenticity, that clamor is subdued.

Adopting authenticity entails putting truth above popularity and content over looks. Instead of striving for perfection, it is a return to the naked, fearless self. Although it is not flawless, the finished sculpture is robust and has depth, consistency, and subtle strength. The blacksmith is aware that heat is necessary for transformation. These are the very forces that make identity visible, not dangers to it. The result of the fire is not something novel, but rather something authentic, tempered, and undeniably true. Walking through discomfort is sometimes a prerequisite to embracing one's true self; doing so often means shedding false layers of fear, expectation, and imitation.

Each strike that takes away what should not belong reveals more of what truly is. "*Authenticity is not found but created in struggle, clarity, and decision.*" Roughness, sharp edges, and uneven strokes may initially appear to be a defect. But as time passes, we develop a new perspective. What was formerly chaotic takes on significance. Every wound, scar, and flaw serve as evidence of a more profound process at work. The hammer's markings are distinct and irreplicable; they are signs of change rather than flaws.

Authenticity cannot flourish in a place where nothing changes or moves. Because what is formed by pressure and truth is not flawless, but it is complete. Authentic living is not a performance. To live honorably means to let the external world mirror the inside reality. No adornment. No disguise. The forged soul, which is sculpted by the clarity of truth rather than by the eyes of others, stands in defense of its pride, just as the blacksmith's honest effort does. It glows with the brilliance of reality rather than modeling itself in borrowed reflections.

5.2 THE PERSONALITY BLUEPRINT: CRAFTING YOUR CORE VALUES

The blacksmith sketches his next creation not on paper but only in his mind. The metal he can work with has potential, but without a plan, there is no result. *Like any strong structure, every resilient personality starts with a blueprint.*" This internal framework was not meant to be decorative; *the words needed to anchor behavior, decision, and action.*

The intention is more than lines and symbols; it is a blueprint. Core values are the blueprint to identity, the stuff to be protected, the things that are worthy of fighting for and letting go. They are chosen, not inherited. They guide the code of conduct and dictate the response to action. All is according to plan in the forge. The blacksmith doesn't strike at random; his blows are methods that suit an imagined structure. *If there are no values, action is random; with them, each choice counts.*"These values must be known and lived through consistent behavior.

Values reveal themselves only if they are tested, not if they are just spoken. The blueprint keeps a person from falling into the path of heat and noise. Repetition engraves the values into instinct. When the framework exists, decisions become easier. It is as much a rhythm practice for the blacksmith as the last decision, and each reinforces the foundation.

The blueprint also evolves, not in its integrity, but in its clarity. As experience deepens, values sharpen. What truly matters reveals itself under pressure or shifting priorities from superficial to substantial. "*The values are no longer a concept; they are known as being.*' The original is still visible, not in ink, but in form, in the final shape of the forged creation. But values creates a personality that would not be won or lost by trends; rather, a personality constructed for resilience. To be seen and served is a stunning, indestructible, and finest creation of the blacksmith.

Nelson Mandela did not seek retribution against anyone despite his 27-year prison sentence. He decided on forgiveness, unity, and dignity. Those weren't just impulsive acts; they mirrored what he believed most deeply, which he had practiced for many years. His behavior came from his unshifting principles, not life's events. Similarly, Ruth Bader Ginsburg, an iconic

American lawyer and jurist, built her life and career on the principles of equality, perseverance, and justice. She consistently adhered to these values in all her hearings, including whenever she disagreed with the majority. Their example shows us that who you are is only partly based on your personality. You have the rest to do. The Personality Blueprint invites you to assess your core beliefs and align them with your actions. Living up to your beliefs can change the world and result in daily, long-lasting benefits.

5.3 THE MAGNETISM OF UNIQUENESS: STANDING OUT IN A CROWD

The blacksmith picks one piece from various pieces as the forge glows softly. In all its imperfections, the handpicked piece, with strange angles and markings, differentiates itself from others. Not despite the differences, the blacksmith smiles. In a world of sameness, the distinctive stands out, attracting admiration and drawing attention.

Uniqueness is not manufactured. It is revealed. That's not to *'stand out'* but to be more truly oneself, not louder. Those who wear masks conform to patterns shaped by fear and societal norms. However, genuine or authentic presence involves appreciating individuality without apology. Performance does not create magnetism. It is born of alignment. Power emerges quietly, powerful, undeniable, unforced, deeply attractive when identity and action fit. Uniqueness glows like a flame that doesn't shout but cannot be ignored.

Not every edge is smoothed by the blacksmith; some are purposefully kept in place as reminders rather than flaws. A silent tale of fortitude and perseverance, each scar and peculiarity in the metal becomes a trademark of the voyage. When viewed in the proper context, the characteristics that others may attempt to conceal become symbols of bravery and moral fiber. People are drawn to honesty and what feels authentic, not to perfection. Standing out requires taking a chance and being open to being noticed, even if that difference causes opposition before it is acknowledged. However, the forge imparts a timeless lesson; pressure fortifies the finished shape. Personality is no different in this regard. The more it is put to the test, the more it solidifies into something happy just to be and not anxious to fit in.

In a world full of noise and imitation, it's easy to get lost trying to be heard. But real strength doesn't shout. It speaks through confidence. Remember that truth endures in silence. Those who understand what sets them apart do not seek attention, but they earn respect. If others are looking for attention, the truly unique ones attract attention because they are rooted, focused, and real. Greatness is not handed to those who shout the loudest; instead, it is drawn to those born to shine. Uniqueness has the power. It does not beg to be seen. It simply shines.

5.4 THE ART OF CONNECTION: BUILDING RELATIONSHIPS

Two pieces of metal unite in the heat of the forge, not by overwhelming one another but by joining together for a common purpose. Metals interact to form bonds rather than to break. Similarly, genuine connection aims for mutual respect, depth, and alignment rather than perfection. "*The best relationships are not just built to look right, but they are shaped to work, endure, and matter effectively.*"In the forge's heat, two metal pieces become one not by overpowering, but by connecting with a purpose. Metal interacts with metal, not to break but to bond. In the same way, authentic connection is not about perfection but about aiming for depth, alignment, and mutual respect.

The art of connection is like the work of a blacksmith, Each metal hits between the fingers of care and the hands of wisdom. If the blacksmith holds it too tight, the bond breaks; if the blacksmith holds it too loose, it falls apart. The real balance lies in authenticity, mutual respect, and patience. Before forging meaningful bonds, the material being used must be solid.

A fragile sense of self also bends under pressure, like fragile metal does. Strong connections are not built overnight. Trust is welded on an honest moment. Just as in metal, the connection hardens from the heat, is shaped by the pressure, and is proven through honesty. Misalignment leads to friction in both people and metal. Knowing this, the blacksmith must make necessary adjustments, cool it, and try again. "*It takes patience, understanding, and commitment to growth to shape lasting relationships.*"

In a world where people are obsessed with being heard, very few take a chance to be heard. In genuine connection, silence itself holds a meaning. One tool is born alone another is created to be used in conjunction with others. Respect and alignment of values lead to synergy and unison. To build an effective relationship, one should honor the differences between the two sides; they are not obstacles but real starting points. Agreement is not the building block of depth; depth is not built on agreement, but on being present with one another in truth. There can be conflict, but where respect is the foundation, the sparks will never harm but will build strength. The blacksmith lays firm and lasting pieces. "*Things that truly matter is not demanded; they endure time, pressure, and distance.*" The forge teaches more than how to shape metal; it teaches how to hold and let go with wisdom, and similarly, in relationship, as in craft, strength is born.

During his most famous years, the adored American television anchor Fred Rogers reminded people that genuine empathy and being present are the keys to true connection. He once remarked that "*Appreciating people means that we are doing the job of God*." His genuine and kind demeanor made his show appeal to a wide range of audiences, providing not only amusement but also a timeless lesson in empathy, acceptance, and emotional intelligence. Likewise, Michelle Obama has made it clear through her actions, both as First Lady and afterward, that close, real connections matter. It all comes down to being genuine, paying attention, and appreciating interpersonal interactions. The connections we build can endure and be founded on trust, respect, and the best aspects of humanity if we lead with sincerity and transparency.

5.5 THE MASTERPIECE OF YOU: LIVING A LIFE THAT REFLECTS YOUR ESSENCE

You are intended to be a canvas, molded by the outlines of your soul and smeared with the hues of your truth, rather than a replica. Living a life that embodies who you are means acting with quiet conviction and allowing your inner self to be heard through your decisions, presence, and journey. Every moment is a stroke toward wholeness, every joy is a flash of light, and every scar creates texture in this living work.

The forge grows quiet. What once roared with heat and spark rests hardened, tempered as the final product. In the form, it bears not only its form but its meaning. A masterpiece is not just built with skill, but it contains a soul. When we live a life of intention, the truth is revealed, our values are entrenched, and our routine is surpassed. You cannot create a masterpiece in haste. The heat, noise, and adjustment matter every moment in the forge. "*Your identity is not a quick creation, but a steady formation over time.*"

Each word, each action is a mark in the character portrait. Choices become brushstrokes. Relationships become the shading; challenges become the texture. There is no copy of anyone else, only a singular story. The blacksmith has his limits, but mastery means knowing the time to strike and to step back and allow the work to speak. Living as a masterpiece means knowing what to say, when to act, and when to remain silent. Expression does not always require excess. It requires presence. An absolute masterpiece requires no explanation; the finished piece speaks for itself. Its form tells its journey.

A well-forged life apologizes for nothing since its essence is reflected in it. It doesn't wear a mask nor strive to impress; it is only resonance. A masterpiece is never accidental. "*It's the result of repeated commitment to the truth.*"This is not an easy way to live, but it is a more meaningful one. After the hammering stops, the impact of the hammer continues. The work remains alive; the forge is at rest. "*The masterpiece of you is not about who you are but how you live. That, above all, is what makes them unforgettable.*"

CHAPTER 6

THE TOOLS OF LEADERSHIP – CRAFTING INFLUENCE

INTRODUCTION

The blacksmith in the forge, where metal finds its purpose, chooses his tools not for function but for their purpose. These instruments have been shaped, perfected, and proven in use. The same goes for leadership tools, sharpened by theory, fire, resistance, and repetition. "*Leadership doesn't topple from a title or position. It flows from being able to influence, uplift, and deliver outcomes with clarity and precision.*"

Great leaders are like good artisans. They carefully envision what they are building and execute it according to the purpose. They do not strike at random; every move is deliberate, and each tool is selected purposefully for the possible task. Influence is not achieved in one blow or one action. It is the result of a series of actions congruent to core values, intentional actions combined over time. For someone who is already a good leader, leading is like forging; it takes perseverance, patience, and a dedication to continuous improvement to shape raw potential.

There is no room for deception in the forge. A tool either proves itself or it doesn't. "*Authenticity is the cornerstone of leadership: where our words align with our actions, and vision follows execution*." If the tools do not work under pressure, they are discarded. In the same way, "*Shallow leadership crumbles when its rein is questioned.*" Only those who have undergone pressure can and will lead others through it.

The hands of balance guide authentic leadership, not brute strength rooted in decisiveness, tempered with empathy, and carried with confidence, balanced by humility. The best leaders are leaders who can strike and listen and decide if they need to go to the front and lead or stand back gracefully. "*Tools become extensions of intent, and leaders become extensions of purpose*." The leadership forge has each tool with a different role in mind. The hammer of vision establishes direction. Empathy is an anchor of strength that absorbs weight and transfers it. They shape results together, which continue regardless of the leader's presence. Measure of influence is not the moments of command, but rather of those whose influence comes into being.

No born leader walks out of there with a whole toolkit. Every skill and every tool are earned through testing, refinement, and time. They are not ornaments; decision-making, vision-setting, and emotional intelligence are skills. Forcing them takes time, and it must be done with wisdom. "*Leadership is never built easily, but in the fire, as one goes through tension, pressure, and unshakable commitment to growth*." The blacksmith does not rest at the end of the day because the work is finished, but because the craft is progressing. So, it is the same with leadership: "*The shaping never stops*." The hand must always remain steady; the tools must always be sharpened. The influence is not claimed in one instance; it is cultivated over a lifetime of consistent, skillful action and intentional influence.

6.1 THE LEADERSHIP TOOLKIT: ESSENTIAL SKILLS FOR EVERY LEADER

In a blacksmith's workshop, all tools with a specific function are kept within arm's reach, chosen for their purpose, proven by their use, and valued for their legacy. None are ornamental, and their utility earns them their place. Like craftsmanship, leadership is also a toolkit that builds not just status but also the skill. Tools are not what make the blacksmith; however, without them, nothing is shaped.

The tools of a leader are not merely tactics; they are systems of principle and motion that have been honed through trial and error and time. Clarity is the ability to speak with purpose, handle emotion gracefully, and maintain focus on what can be rather than merely what is. This is what truly possesses power. These are thoughtful reactions rather than impetuous ones, in which the actions are in line with the truth, and silences that are maintained out of concern rather than fear.

When a great leader is in charge, communication is more than sound. It hits like a hammer, and every word is measured for a purpose; it either shapes or breaks the shared vision. "*Words serve as chisels, not fillers. They set expectations, provide guidance, and validate purpose.*" They define rather than adorn. Precision is power in a leader's toolbox because every decision, every pause, and every communication have an impact on the project being produced.

The file of self-discipline lies beside the hammer, like a quiet, steady, and essential factor. The hammer delivers the force, and the file refines the edges. Together, they create not just outcomes but also the leader behind them. Consistency is a silent hero in leadership, a repetition earned, not charisma. A leader who listens captures that trust more quickly than one who gives commands.

Empathy is not a weakness; it is a precision tool that reaches the foundation of all things. At a temperature, metal changes, and so must the hand that forms it. Building on this idea, lasting leadership does the unexpected without compromising its core values. In changing circumstances, the leader's strength lies in seeing change not as a threat but as new material to work with and shape into something more substantial.

The blacksmith takes the tools in hand daily, checks them up, oils them, files them, and handles them carefully. The same applies to leaders; *they must reflect, improve, and be teachable.* No tool sharpens itself. For any skill to remain effective, it must be practiced regularly and tested through experience. The tools in the forge come to nothing more substantial than the hands that hold them. It is not from the tools we have but from learning how to use them, when and how, that leadership grows.

6.2 THE VISIONARY'S HAMMER: CRAFTING A CLEAR AND COMPELLING FUTURE

The blacksmith in the quiet forge lifts the hammer not to finish but to begin. The end must be visualized in the mind before the first strike lands, as we know that vision always comes before the commencement of work. "*The first act of a leader is vision, pulling the future close enough to manipulate through any tool.'The hammer does not guess; each one drives in a direction.* Without vision, leadership is merely noise, and without rhythm, it is even more so. The hammer swings, but no shape forms. "*A clear vision creates a purpose; each word, action, and effort is shaped by intention and direction.*"

The blacksmith does not stop in the middle of the strike; likewise, a visionary leader keeps the team moving with steady momentum aligned to a shared direction or goal. Vision is not vague. Though specific, it must be bold enough to inspire. "*Vision with clarity chisels confusion from the path, leaving a clear path for the followers to* *follow with the hang of their feet.'*Leaders see beyond the surface to possibility and turn the greatest futures into realities.

Shaping metal does not exhaust the visionary's hammer; it binds material to purpose. The leader anticipates the future when others' imaginations are limited, and he swings into rhythm until belief is distributed. Vision does not work alone. It must be repeated, refined, and reinforced. *'A vision not often whispered becomes forgotten.''*It is the leader's job to instill it in the foundation until it resonates in every task and every decision. In storms of doubt, vision is the anchor held together by the clarity of the destination; the forge lights up when outcomes delay and results falter.

Vision is the light that guides the way through the darker night and gives a constant heading to go when the path changes. The first strike out of the blacksmith's horn will be its shape. First, a vision that leads to leadership, but then discipline and clarity make it sustainable.

6.3 THE EMPATHY ANVIL: LEADING WITH HEART AND UNDERSTANDING

Authentic leadership is formed on the anvil of empathy, not with noise, but with subtlety. It is the silent power that listens before speaking and leans in before taking the lead. Feeling the burden of another person's hardship while maintaining hope is what it means to lead from the heart. It is the art of seeing souls as well as roles and using kind hands to guide complex judgments. Compassion is not a weakness in this type of leadership; rather, it is the steady rhythm that builds trust, the fire that tempers wisdom, and the invisible force that unites people to a common goal.

The anvil bears every strike, holding steady. The blow is absorbed, and the process is brought together. "*Empathy is the anvil of the leader,*" a silent force that absorbs tension and transforms it into resilience. Without empathy, leadership can create harm. With it, the pressure becomes progress. Outstanding leadership does not take place above people but somewhat beside them. "*Empathy grounds leadership in humanity.*" Then, some rare leaders switch logic for empathy, working to translate the names of numbers and performances into people.

The hammer will never break the anvil, no matter how hard it's caught. Empathy is not simple; it is precisely the strength generated by impact. To lead with empathy is to breathe before striking, to slow down, to ask, to listen, and to acknowledge that empathy is a genuine and essential quality. "*Empathic leaders know what is not being said, and they understand what is not observable.*" This type of leadership is neither loud nor showy; It listens before it acts. The anvil holds all kinds of metal, just as authentic leadership holds space for every personality and every story.

Under pressure, empathy reveals real character. When leaders with empathy at their core face situations of conflict or stress, they are not just managing the problem; they are offering a grounded response. "*Empathy transforms conflict into a conversation.*" Just as the iron forge supports creation, the source of empathy also fosters growth. The empathy within the teams allows them to endure more, take more risks, and perform better because they feel seen. The most underutilized instrument is the anvil, which is silent, immobile, and necessary. It doesn't seek attention, but its existence shapes everything. In a similar vein, empathy doesn't demand attention yet has a powerful, understated effect. You should expect depth, influence, and the subtle ability to change rather than noise if you're looking for empathy.

6.4 THE DECISIVE STRIKE: MAKING TOUGH CALLS WITH CONFIDENCE

The blacksmith must give a clean strike at critical moments of need. In leadership, that moment is decisive, the point at which preparation meets action. The metal will be even more decisive than the artist; the wrong strike will spoil the piece. Leadership involves choice. Not every strike is going to be a perfect one, but everyone must be taken. "*It is not about always being right, but it is about never being unclear.*"

The team under good leadership does not require constant agreement to work well; they need clarity. The decisive strike waits for preparation rather than reaction and is never hurried. When ideals are sculpted from vision and bravely guarded, there are no "*Tough Calls*." A leader needs to know when the time is right, just like the blacksmith who won't lift the hammer until he is certain. Even if it is silent, delay erodes trust. Every choice and action is a step closer to the goal, not for the sake of power, but for the fulfillment of a purpose.

Errors could ensue. It is a component of the forge. It takes mistakes to become a leader. The heat of change is contained within every mistake. Where the process is improved, growth starts, and new leadership arises from that crucible. A leader must pay attention to the stroke, sense the strain, and make deliberate adjustments, much like the blacksmith at the anvil. In addition, resolute leaders offer stability by giving directions to their team.

When doubt creeps in for a team or individual, their leader's assurance acts like a light. Bold and calculated decisions generate momentum, especially when the future is unknown and others are reluctant to move. Although they don't address every query, they offer suggestions on how to do so. In the silence before the strike, the forge waits. The blow is with precision, and everything changes. "*One clear decision made with courage can change the course of everything*."

6.5 THE LEGACY OF LEADERSHIP: INSPIRING OTHERS TO FOLLOW YOUR PATH

Authentic leadership is not just measured by titles held or milestones reached, but by the lasting influence it leaves behind. The work doesn't settle easily; when the forge cools and the tools are set down, something remains, not just the job but the impact. "*Authentic leadership outlives its presence.*"Legacy begins long before departure. It is formed in mundane things, unheeded help, and comfort.

Leadership walked the path as it is today and laid the foundation for the path's others will walk tomorrow. Commands are not the most significant source of influence for a leader, but rather for his character model. Human leadership is not carved in stone; it is planted in people.

The legacy of leadership is not just forged in a single moment; it is built slowly with integrity, service, and a relentless vision. It's crafted with the same patience, faith, and care that all blacksmiths' masterpieces are. The most durable legacies are made up of stories that are lived, told, and remembered rather than being made of stone. Leaders who have a team at their side are aware of this fact: when we tackle a challenge collectively, no storm is too big or road too unpredictable. Possibilities become infinite in unity. "*Leadership makes an impact that lasts not for authority, but impact*." Every act becomes a chapter. A true legacy multiplies. It gives the fire to others to rise, to lead, to pass to those who will rise and lead.

When Dr. Martin Luther King Jr. led the march in Selma, he embodied justice rather than merely discussing it. Leading was not about giving orders but about leading by example, so people followed willingly. He explained, "*An honest leader builds consensus rather than looking for it*."

Similarly, as a teenager, Malala Yousafzai demonstrated that leading from genuine conviction is more effective than leading from age or rank. Despite fear and threats, the movement to stand up for girls' learning sparked an international effort. They make it clear that leading is not only about having power over others. It's about setting a goal, acting, and having a positive impact on those around us. When you lead by doing what's right and loving your mission, many others are more inspired to do the same. If you set a good example, not only do you get to your objective, but you also encourage others to improve.

CHAPTER 7

THE MASTERPIECE MINDSET – POLISHING YOUR LEGACY

INTRODUCTION

Every soul possesses the spark to create the extraordinary, not just to exist, but to construct a life that echoes beyond its years. Many people drift through time, mistaking their days for occasional moments, unaware that they are creating something timeless. The Masterpiece Mindset, which sees life as a living painting in which every experience is a texture, every choice is a deliberate brushstroke, and every breath is a note in the composition of being in the awakening. This sculpture is sacred, not a pointless digression. A meaningful life is one in which each decision we make, every action we take, and each silent heartbeat we make contributes to the picture of who we are supposed to be.

The masterpiece mindset is, at its core, about the practice of intentional living. This philosophy encourages people to live their actions in line with their core values and make decisions that reflect the person they aspire to be, rather than the person they are at that moment. Like an artist who plans, tinkers, and polishes his work, we are the artists of our own lives. "*The true beauty of a masterpiece does not lie in its perfection but in the honesty, effort, and authenticity poured into it.*" Refusing to live life on autopilot is a sign of having this masterpiece mindset.

However, it necessitates presence, consciousness, and a distinct sense of purpose. This begins by asking the right questions, such as: "*What legacy do I want to leave*?" and "*What impact do I want my life to make in the world around me?*" No matter how seemingly moderate, every decision you make adds up in time and will make a legacy that lasts more than a lifetime.

A masterpiece is not made in a day, but a well-lived life does not develop. It is made by consistency, persistence and discipline while having the courage to face life's challenges. The Masterpiece Mindset is a mindset of growth, resilience, and continuous improvement. It allows us to look at past obstacles as an opportunity to refine our character, vision, and purpose. Every setback is part of becoming something more; an artist considers imperfections part of the journey.

To live intentionally, you need to design a life that embodies your values and recognize the powerful influence your actions have on the world. Not only is this a call to live with purpose, but such a call means that every day is a chance to bring your masterpiece closer to completion. Like a piece of metal in the forge, life can be shaped and refined into something extraordinary. "*The outcome is not even the point; it's a process of creating a masterpiece.*'

The masterpiece mindset is learning that life's value lies not in perfection but in taking intentional action, applying the principles of consistency and clarity to one's purpose. Like a blacksmith forms the iron with strength and patience, so must we create our lives with audacity and claws. If these values are already in the heart, the blueprint is ready; then it is time to put these values into words and polish them through every action, every decision, and every relationship. As we progress, we are on the path to building our legacy. "*Every step count, every effort is a blow of the hammer, and each pain is an opportunity to create something that lasts*."

7.1 THE MASTERPIECE PHILOSOPHY: LIFE AS A WORK OF ART

Life is a glorious masterpiece and a canvas worthy of being filled with all the intention, beauty, and depth we offer. In this context, *'Living a meaningful life'* means working purposely and thoughtfully as if an artist is working on canvas. When we adopt the philosophy of life as art, it leads us to look at life through the eyes of art, causing us to see the small things that would otherwise go unnoticed; every experience in our life is part of the picture of how our story is put together.

Like any work of art, life is messy, and it includes mistakes, revisions, and unexpected turns the artist had not planned for. So, too, is life. Based on this, greatness is not perfected in beauty but in the humbling moments of struggle, design, and skill. The imperfections, the setbacks, and the challenges all contribute to the beauty of the finished work. Our hardships are not obstacles but opportunities to mature our character and gain greater knowledge. Like a picture, life develops in brushstrokes that stray from perfection, each line quivering with purpose despite its imperfections. Even when the brush defies the hand, something genuine shows through a beauty that is not limited to symmetrical or admired by the eye that is only trained on the expected. The smudge has grace, the uneven colour has meaning, and the bits that do not fit have truth. In time and tenderness, what some could refer to as error becomes the piece's core.

Life finds its art in what dares to be honest, raw, and undone, not in what is perfect, just as a canvas life through its flaws. Intentional choice is the key to living life as a work of art. Just as an artist chooses colours and strokes, we ought to select values, relationships, and actions. Intentional living is not being caught up in life but instead living a life you choose to be a part of. You must engage in personal management; you can consciously shape your destiny by aligning your daily actions with what is deeply rooted within you. Masterpieces require patience. The artist has no rush process because every layer and detail hold meaning. "*Commitment to the process brings true artistry*."

In the same way, life demands patience from us when we should either forgive or grow, evolve, or forgive ourselves. If we chase excellence, we know that some things will unfold slowly and by chance. Happiness comes from becoming, not from achieving. The concept of authenticity forms the core of the philosophy of life as a masterpiece. "*Authenticity gives birth to a true masterpiece; it is like an artist's inner truth brought to the surface.*" Similarly, the life we create should align with the true essence of our being. It is easy to be steered by external forces or to follow the leader, but the true beauty in a well-lived life is living to the fullest capacity, with awareness and purpose, according to one's values and desires. To leave as a work of art means to become both creator and creator. This is about living our lives to the fullest, with awareness and purpose, so that our lives will be a legacy that represents the absolute beauty of our journey.

7.2 THE LEGACY MAP: DESIGNING A LIFE THAT MATTERS

Life is a journey characterized by choices, actions, and values that define an individual. Like an artist drawing a masterpiece, one must first purposefully chart and design one's life. Accumulating achievements is not creating a legacy; rather, it is about accumulating craft during your lifetime. A legacy map starts with direction clarity. For this reason, you must first decide where you want to build a meaningful existence. First, it all comes down to figuring out what matters most.

One must gather their ideals and passions before starting any major trip. Every choice is directed by an internal compass, which brings clarity to complicated issues, when success is determined by a person's alignment with a distinct purpose rather than by what society believes. When crafting a legacy, take a step back and reflect on yourself. Ask yourself, "*What do you want to be remembered for?*" "*What have you wished to leave behind?*"The legacy map invites you to live with intention, design with purpose, and act with integrity. There will be situations in which the road breaks down, and we find ourselves uncertain, the destination obscured by haze.

Nevertheless, we continue to move not by sight, but by intention, by following a map that is not depicted in terms of results but rather in terms of daily decisions. This map is a compass for life, a quiet rhythm beneath the cacophony, not a finish line. Every choice we make, no matter how minor, contributes to the larger picture and tells a tale that reverberates beyond our own. We set the foundation for a legacy with every action, whether it's caring for someone you love, giving your gift bravely, or pursuing a passion that serves a bigger good rather than just yourself. The gradual art of becoming, rather than big arrivals, is where life finds purpose.

Our life journey is full of challenges, but it should never make us stray from the map. *Resilience is built on each roadblock.'*Obstacles are for good; they teach us a lesson, refine our character, and often redirect us toward our true purpose. It is about seeing these challenges as necessary aspects of the design process rather than obstacles to success. Secondly, when problems arise, the legacy map helps us become more resilient and adaptable and learn from every experience.

Another key point in designing a life that matters is being able to be flexible. The map is a guide, but life is unpredictable, and conditions may have to change along the way. "*The map is not a static entity; it changes, depending on circumstances, the perspective and the understanding of its interpretation.*" It is necessary to change the map as new opportunities arise and contribute to who you are becoming. Ultimately, no life matters if it is not also a life that enriches others in a way that sustains the world. If you stick to the outlined legacy map, you will establish a life that satisfies you and something that'll be forever etched in the world.

7.3 THE POLISH OF PURPOSE: ALIGNING YOUR ACTIONS WITH YOUR VALUES

There is no such thing as a masterpiece struck in one stroke, nor is one's life transformed in a single moment. An artist must prepare their work well so that careful polishing will reveal its true brilliance. We must also align our actions with our values and lead a life of purpose. Purpose is the polish that emphasizes our actions and character and makes them extraordinary or ordinary. Living a purpose means deciding what we do and choosing our actions, which aligns with our core values. Without this alignment, we can become committed to living from the outside instead of the inside. "*When your actions are rooted in your values, life is no longer a string of disconnected moments; it is the unfolding of a life lived with authenticity and purpose.*"

Our purpose is grounded in the values that guide us in the face of complex challenges. Without them, we are shipwrecked, out to sea, at the mercy of the waves of destiny, unsure of how to move. One of the hardest things to do in life is to match actions with values. Ultimately, the world provides distractions, shortcuts, and outside pressure to purchase things despite our moral principles. For instance, artists must fight the temptation to cut corners or rush their work, and we must uphold our morals even in the face of inconvenience.

There is no inconvenience in purpose. It is the action of sticking to what is essential because your principles demand no less. Growth results from making decisions that represent the person one wants to become rather than the version society expects one to be. This alignment begins with self-reflection. It is about asking whether each step aligns with what is valued most deeply and being open to change when it does not. Just as an artist step back to their work from different angles, people must pause and evaluate their lives. "*Purpose comes from consistency in choices, actions, beliefs, and the willingness to adjust.*" This reflection of a purpose for our life helps us to keep life on track with what truly matters. When our life is guided by a purpose, we will feel that things are more in sync.

When our actions align with values, decisions become lighter, and our days become clearer. The reduction in internal conflicts would create a more satisfying life. Each step feels honest, real, and reflective of something bigger than the moment itself. The purpose is not something to reach once; it is a journey. It is a way of moving through life. It is not the finish line; it is the ongoing journey of adjusting actions to match what truly matters. It is what turns the ordinary into something meaningful.

When Malala Yousafzai challenged the Taliban over her right to education, it was because she believed in it, not for any fame. From her early days of speaking out as a child to her appearance at the United Nations, she has acted passionately in support of equality and justice. Being clear about what she wanted helped her words travel around the world. Similarly, Yvon Chouinard, a renowned American rock climber and environmentalist, founded Patagonia to support the environment, not just enabling people to go hiking. He made choices for the business that supported the environment, even handing control of the company to an activist organization for the same reason. They remind us that having a purpose is not enough; you must also live it.

You achieve the polish of purpose when your daily work matches your deepest values. It is what helps your goals become real and your thoughts genuine. When you are in alignment, you go further and radiate positive energy. In the end, purpose adds shine to life, just like polish brings out the beauty in a finished masterpiece. It transforms day-to-day into something richer and more intentional. "*Success may fade, but a life guided by purpose endures marked by truth, integrity, and lasting impact.*" Such a life does not shout for attention. It simply shines, and in doing so, it leaves a mark on everyone it touches.

7.4 THE RIPPLE EFFECT: HOW YOUR CHOICES IMPACT THE WORLD

A single drop of water may seem small, but when a blacksmith touches hot iron in the still water, it creates waves that travel far. "*As you make a choice, it ripples outward and creates life in every other person you are connected to in the circle of life.*" What happens in one life does not stay contained; it reaches others and shapes moments, mindsets, and futures. In a world spinning fast, it is easy to lose sight of the small decisions that cause and lead to all negative debacles in life. Even the slightest acts, pledges of integrity, or dismissals disrupt the environment.

Everything counts and carries weight and direction; there are no isolated choices. This ripple effect is not loud. It begins quietly, one decision at a time. Like the wind-shaping rock over centuries, each choice has a lasting influence on relationships, communities, and culture. A leader who chooses to listen instead of control builds trust with his team and stakeholders. A gesture of kindness from a stranger in a tense moment can break down walls. These are not headline-making events, but they are quiet, deliberate movements. "*True change often moves silently, guided by steady conviction rather than noise.*" Results are rarely instant and do not happen overnight.

The seeds of action take time to grow. Some remain hidden for months or years before their effects become apparent. However, growth is happening. The encouragement given in private, values lived out with quiet consistency, or one brave decision rooted in principle, continues long after the moment has passed. "*The most powerful legacy is not always visible immediately. Its impact deepens and keeps growing even in your absence*". This awareness brings responsibility.

Influence is not about position or popularity. It is about living with intention. Actions in private would shape outcomes in public. "*Success is not found in applause, but it is the silent trust earned by doing what is right.*" Knowing this means nothing is neutral. Every moment is a chance to build, break, or heal. The effect might not always be seen, but it is always present. A quiet word of encouragement or a decision to protect what is right. All these shapes the world.

The masterpiece mindset teaches that legacy is not something that's only left behind. It is something that is lived every day. Those aligned with purpose do not need to demand influence. "*They become the source of waves that move through others long after they are gone*." A well-lived life does not shout to be remembered. It speaks through lives touched, choices witnessed, and strength passed forward. That is how a ripple becomes a tide. That is how a legacy is made.

Instead of using a sword, Mahatma Gandhi favoured justice-honed silence, a weapon that was created in peace yet powerful enough to upend entire civilizations. His opposition to British shackles was more than just a call for liberty; it was a moral spark that warmed people's hearts and resonated for years. Not to injure but to awaken, he marched with defiance in his step and salt in his hand.

A revolution enveloped in silence but louder than battle, every act of silent resistance and every refusal to bend was a hymn of civil disobedience performed without a single yell. He demonstrated that only conscience and conviction have power, not force. Gandhi not only supported India's independence but also introduced the world to Nelson Mandela and Martin Luther King Jr. as leaders in the fight for justice. His life proved that one individual's choices, based on truth and peace, despite overwhelming opposition, can change history through the ripple effect.

7.5 THE ETERNAL MASTERPIECE: LEAVING A MARK THAT LASTS

A masterpiece, when complete, speaks for itself. It does not beg for attention or need to explain its worth. Its presence alone commands respect. "*The most enduring legacy is not carved in stone or shouted aloud. It is lived, felt, and quietly passed on.*" What remains is not just the work done, the life behind it, the values, the choices, and the moments that shaped it. It is not the work that is done that remains, but the life that was lived in the back of it.

True legacy is not about fame or recognition. What mattered was being sure that something was built. We had an ally of a word that strengthened, a choice that formed, and a presence that encouraged. "*What is made eternal is not the size of the impact but the truth behind it.*" Extraordinary lives are not always evident, but they are known through the people changed, ideas spread, and principles handed on.

Over time, the message forming into the eternal masterpiece is never created in haste. Meaning has no shortcut. The alignment polices it, and the patience of little things, done repetitively. "*It has nothing to do with reward legacy; it is the natural result of a life defined by conviction.*" The responsibility does not lie in merely being remembered by everyone, but in leaving an unforgettable memory to the right ones for the right reasons. A legacy like that doesn't easily erode.

The integrity of a constructed life cannot be destroyed, even though accolades come and go, titles shift, and trends change. Like iron tested in fire, it stands firm. "*A life shaped by unshakable values does not need to be lifted. It becomes its monument.*" A masterpiece does not need to be in the spotlight. It allows others to rise. It responds when asked, remains silent when required, and leads without hesitation. It is a quiet guide, more about presence than performance. "*Legacy is not about control; it is about building strength in others and giving them space to grow."*

The quintessential Renaissance genius, Leonardo da Vinci, lived not only to grow but also to produce an enduring masterpiece that would endure for centuries. So insatiable was his curiosity that he studied anatomy, engineering, art, and nature to understand the world at its deepest levels, if not for fame. However, the Mona Lisa was not just a painting. The Mona Lisa represented a lifetime's drive for perfection, touched with mystery, precision, and soul. The fact that Leonardo's legacy is proof that you do not have to contribute just one feat to last long but it is all the passion, discipline, and wonder over a lifetime that gets poured into every stroke, every sketch, and every idea. He showed that true immortality lies in our work that continues to inspire us after one is gone.

The most lasting impact comes from the unseen. It is in conversation that gives someone hope. The example is that discipline. The kindness offered without recognition. These things are not forgotten. They live on in stories told, in habits repeated, in lives changed. "*A true masterpiece does not just leave behind an image; it leaves behind a way to live.*" And when it is all said and done, there is no need to announce the end. The story lives on in those who continue walking the path it lit. It does not need a final speech or a farewell. Its presence lingers in others in how they speak, how they lead, and how they choose. "*An eternal masterpiece is not finished when the creator stops. It continues through the lives it helped shape*." That is the mark that truly lasts. Not because it tried to last but because it mattered. Always.

CHAPTER 8

The Eternal Flame – Sustaining Your Growth

INTRODUCTION

A flame cannot ignite spontaneously, nor can it persist without attention. It starts tiny, delicate, and vulnerable, and needs care and purpose to survive. It soon fades if no one is around to nourish it. However, that flame changes when it is managed. It turns into a lighthouse and a wellspring of coziness, warmth, and memory. We discover presence, heritage, and significance in its radiance in addition to light. Personal development is similar. It doesn't come with a big show or a parade. Unlike other activities that sparkle for a short time, it is not ostentatious or noisy.

Growth is consistent. It's intentional. It takes time and patience. When change is genuine and long-lasting, it takes time to occur. It develops gradually and becomes an enduring aspect of who we are. Examining the eternal flame serves as a reminder of the value of lifelong learning and steady advancement. Half-hearted endeavors or sporadic effort never led to a fulfilling existence. Instead, it is developed over many years by discipline, hard work, and a steadfast dedication to progress.

We must review our objectives, hone our character, and recommit our course, much as the blacksmith repeatedly shapes iron by heating and pressing it back into the fire. The strength of our flame is our progress; our purpose likewise only lasts when we make the daily decision to keep it going. *"Growth doesn't flourish in ease; it's born from friction and fueled by the choices that keep the flame alive.*" Habits become fuel and reflection becomes the air and the purpose, the heat. Together, they keep the fire burning. But Growth isn't a solo act.

Just like a fire is best kept with the help of others, personal Growth is supported by connection, challenge, and wisdom. It must be earned through experience, effort, and honest commitment. The flame isn't fed by noise or attention but by value and purpose. The goal isn't to rise quickly but to remain. To remain curious and to remain focused and committed. When purpose sparks the flame, it must be protected. And when protected, that light does more than guide the way; it becomes the story left behind. "*While growth improves the future, it also brightens up the past that has been left behind.*"

8.1 THE ETERNAL FLAME FRAMEWORK: COMMITTING TO LIFELONG GROWTH

The flame inside the forge flickers and rises peacefully in the back of the room. Even as times change, there is always at least one spark that remains. This growing flame shows the process of lifelong growth. "*True transformation isn't built on bursts of intensity; it's built on the quiet consistency that doesn't wear out.*" Growth isn't about a quick spark. It's about staying lit, day after day, with purpose and care. The eternal flame doesn't just spark growth; it ignites it. It becomes the act of growing. Its first and strongest fuel is purpose. Without purpose, progress loses direction. A flame without a wick wanders, flares, and dies.

Purpose anchors growth. It tells what matters and why it matters. "*When growth is tied to meaning, it becomes natural, not forced.*" Living with intention means choosing what deserves effort and what needs to be left behind. Every fire needs a reason to burn. The second fuel is discipline. The purpose may light up the match, but discipline keeps the fire alive. Lasting change doesn't come from rare bursts of effort. It comes from steady, daily steps.

Discipline brings structure, and structure offers freedom when used with purpose. When a routine reflects values, it becomes a powerful guide, not a trap. The third element is reflection. Without it, action can become aimless. Honest self-awareness and feedback help keep the flame steady. "*Growth that listens, adapts, and becomes stronger. It doesn't break.*"

Reflection brings clarity. It reveals what fuels the fire and what weakens it. The third fuel is the environment. Fire cannot thrive in the cold. Growth thrives in spaces that have the tension of challenge and the safety of support. The right people, surroundings, and influences either stir or smother the flame. "*Growth comes from within, but it must be protected and encouraged from the outside, too.*" A strong environment speaks life, delivers truth, and pushes limits. It helps the flame stay strong when doubt creeps in. Finally, Growth needs resilience. The flame will be tested. Winds will blow, setbacks will come, and progress will feel invisible. But these trials are where endurance is built. "*The flame that survives the storm becomes unshakable.*"

Even when results are unclear, continuing is the true sign of lifelong Growth. The eternal flame framework, built on purpose, discipline, reflection, environment, and resilience, doesn't promise ease. It promises depth. Growth is not about doing more but becoming more aligned with the truth. "*To commit to lifelong growth is to believe that the best version of yourself is never finished. It's always evolving.*"Though the fire may sometimes sway and dim, it endures through care and consistency. When protected, it becomes something more than personal; it becomes a beacon for others to follow.

8.2 THE GROWTH FORGE: LEARNING AND EVOLVING EVERY DAY

Inside the forge, the metal is always in motion. It is in motion, shaped by heat, hammered with purpose, and slowly transformed from a rough block into something valuable. Growth works in the same way. It's not a single event but a continuous cycle of becoming. *"Growth is evolution, the ongoing process of being reshaped by every obstacle, every lesson in every day*." The first step in the growth forge is discomfort. Just as the blacksmith must heat the metal until it softens, real Growth begins when comfort is left behind. It happens when things get hard, routines are disrupted, and uncertainty forces us to adapt and stretch. "*Growth doesn't come without pressure. It's forged into a challenge.*" In discomfort, potential comes to life. It's a space where something new can be created.

Next comes focused effort. The blacksmith doesn't swing his hammer without aim. Every strike matters. The same principle applies to personal growth. Progress comes through intention and daily decisions that align with purpose. "*Those who strike with purpose move forward. Those who wait for change to find them stay still.*" Each habit, each choice, even the smallest step, adds value to the bigger picture. Repetition builds strength. Repetition builds excellence.

Then comes adaptability. Not every tool fits every job. Sometimes, adjustments are necessary. Growth demands the same flexibility. When a path no longer works, it must be changed. Mistakes are not roadblocks but lessons. When viewed as teachers, they offer direction. The willingness to shift, learn, and evolve continues the forward movement. Another powerful element of growth is curiosity.

The blacksmith doesn't adhere to a single way of doing things. He explores new methods, tests new materials, and refines his crafts. "*Growth is fueled by curiosity: each question becomes a spark that lights our path ahead.*" Knowledge only comes from questions. Being curious helps you discover new ideas, perspectives, and a deeper meaning in relationships, careers, and personal growth. Lastly, there is reflection. The blacksmith leans in, his hands still warm from the fire recollection, as the hammer becomes quiet. He raises the object he moulded out of sweat and spark, examines its shape beneath the soot, and tests its edge against the silence. He examines with patience what needs to be brightened, what needs to be smoothed, and where the flame needs to touch again—not to destroy, but to refine. Growth requires the same pause.

Without reflection, actions become motion without meaning. "*Reflection turns activity into wisdom.*" It helps reveal what's working, what's not, and how to move forward more clearly and purposefully. The growth forge is never finished. It doesn't stop after a single breakthrough. It continues daily, challenge by challenge and lesson by lesson. "*To commit to learning and evolving every day is to promise that tomorrow will be stronger, wiser, and better than today.*" Like the metal that leaves the forge stronger and more refined, Growth shapes people into something more. Not perfect, but purposeful. Not finished, but ready. Ready to step into the next challenge, fueled by experience, shaped by effort, and lit by the fire of constant Growth.

Elon Musk exists at the forefront of technology and innovation because, at some point or another throughout his career, he has occupied the relentless heat of the growth forge. In this place, you have to learn and evolve, or you have to die. Musk never based his technique on traditional education, from when he taught himself rocket science to when he launched SpaceX. On the contrary, though, he soaked up information and quickly adapted, taking leaps of faith that the others wouldn't. Every rocket explosion and every Tesla production delay was a lesson that drew him and his organization closer to it. His path shows that growth is less about getting it all right now and more about growing towards audacious definitions of goals by learning faster, thinking deeper, and adapting consistently.

8.3 THE SUSTAINED GROWTH TRACKER: MEASURING YOUR PROGRESS OVER TIME

With the aid of the *Sustained Growth Tracker,* you may monitor your development over time in a consistent manner, identifying both your areas of improvement and those that require improvement. Small, continuous victories help you stay on track with long-term objectives and promote deliberate development via introspection and modification. Pursuing growth is not a finish line. This journey is a continuous process. But without a way to track that journey, it's easy to feel lost or discouraged. Like a blacksmith who uses tools to measure and refine his work, Growth also needs structure. "*What gets measured gets better*." Knowing how far you've come depends on knowing where you're going.

The first step in building a sustained growth tracker is setting clear, actionable goals. Without goals, progress becomes hard to see. Goals work like a map; they show where to begin, where to head, and when to adjust. "*In the forge of life, our goals shape the path forward*." Practical goals follow the *SMART model: Specific, Measurable, Attainable, Relevant, and Time-bound*. These goals provide direction for each step and turn every success or failure into valuable information. Once goals are set, the next step is tracking small wins.

Growth doesn't happen at all at once. It's made up of small, consistent efforts over time. "*A journey of a thousand miles is walked in thousands of small steps*." So, we should have the courage to show up on hard days, enjoy learning something new, and create a mindset to bounce back from mistakes. These moments might seem small, but they prove that growth is happening even when it's not apparent.

Another powerful tool in tracking progress is feedback. Just as a blacksmith examines his creation and polishes weak spots, Growth also needs review. Feedback helps reveal what's working and what needs adjustment. "*Feedback is the mirror that shows both strength and weakness*." Receiving honest feedback from others and conducting self-evaluation allows you to refine your process and clarify your course. Failure is not a sign to stop. Instead, it is a sign to learn. Feedback, combined with teaming up and reflection, helps. Growth isn't just about moving forward; it's also about pausing and taking the time to reflect. So, "*Reflection is what we make of experience*."

We can only genuinely move forward by looking back. Reflection enables you to see the whole picture, teaches you about past efforts, and helps you adjust your path. It keeps you on track with your values and long-term vision. Even the best effort can go off track without reflection.

Finally, and most importantly, a robust growth tracker consists of celebrating milestones. In all, its small or large achievements deserve recognition. These moments matter whether you complete a goal or stay consistent. Of course, movement and celebration both fuel progress. Milestones help maintain momentum and remind you that the journey is worthwhile. "*By tracking your progress, you make progress.*" Define what you want to have. Take note of the small wins. Give ear to feedback. Reflect for a while. There is no shame in celebrating how far you've come. But it is more than building progress. It is confidence-building. It disciplines people. Slowly, step by step, it leads you to become the strongest, most honest version of yourself.

8.4 THE FIREKEEPERS: SURROUNDING YOURSELF WITH INSPIRING PEOPLE

The journey of growth was never meant to be walked alone. Just as a blacksmith depends on skilled hands to help keep the forge burning, personal growth also depends on the people surrounding you. "*The right people can ignite the spark of your potential.*" These firekeepers fuel your ambition, challenge your limits, and keep you on the course when the path gets tough. Behind every strong person, there is a group that inspires and supports that person. "*Sharing our progress with others committed to the same journey generates more fire than when it is done alone.*" It's about finding encouragement and building up that support network around you. These firekeepers can be mentors, friends, teammates, or have brief connections. Most importantly, they push you forward and remind you of your strength. Think of these things as highlighting your character and how you challenge them. Like the assistant at the forge who offers guidance and feedback, these people help refine your path. "*Challenge sharpens the mind, just as pressure strengthens the metal.*"

The firekeepers don't simply agree with everything. They ask hard questions. They push you to stretch beyond your comfort zone. Actual growth becomes real when others encourage you to face your fears, take new steps, and rethink old patterns. Another key trait of firekeepers is their ability to hold you accountable. It's easy to lose direction without someone reminding you of your goals. "*In the forge of life, accountability is the anvil that shapes intentions into actions*."

Firekeepers remind you of your promises. They call out when your effort slips. They check in not to judge but to help. They ensure your journey isn't made up of scattered moments but of clear, committed steps. Just as important is their emotional support. Growth isn't always easy. There are moments when motivation fades, progress stalls, and doubts creep in. Firekeepers help keep your flame alive during those times. "*A well-tended flame needs intensity and stillness to keep burning.*" Whether through a kind word or simply showing up, their presence can reignite passion when it's on the verge of fading.

Maya Angelou, a well-known American poet, singer, and civil rights activist, mentored Oprah Winfrey, who became one of her mentees. Maya helped shape Oprah's purpose and helped keep the flame burning during moments of doubt; Oprah often speaks about how Maya played a crucial role in this. However, these stories also remind us that success is rarely achieved alone. The Firekeepers are the ones who help ignite your passion, call you into confrontations that challenge your thinking, and believe in your vision, for better or worse, even when you're wavering. If you walk around with inspiring people, you don't just stay lit; you also become a light.

Lastly, great firekeepers share alignment. Their dreams may not look like yours, but their values are similar. They believe in the power of purpose, Growth, and effort. They increase your energy multiple times. And you arrive at the next destination much faster, stronger, and with greater purpose together. No flame burns well in the furnace of life alone. Every fire starts with one spark, but a ring of fire can light the world. *Hang around people who will challenge, support, and inspire you.*'Pick firekeepers that aid your light in expanding instead of fading. Personal Growth is not the only type of growth worth striving for. It's powered through a connection. With the right people, though, that fire never dies.

8.5 THE NEVER-ENDING JOURNEY: EMBRACING THE PROCESS OF BECOMING

Growth is not a chore to be finished and put away, nor is it a finish line to be passed. It isn't a place marked by accolades, success, or acclaim. The truth subtly narrates that actual growth does not wait for the end, despite the world's temptation to follow it. Every step of the way is inhaled by it. Growing entails living in the liminal space between who you were and who you will become but completely present in the growing. Therefore, honour the process and let go of the desire to *arrive.* Because there is no end to the journey, only to walk through new chapters, and every page offers the opportunity to grow as a person.

This journey of growth means seeing life as an ongoing process. There's no endpoint. There's always more to learn, more to understand, and more ways to evolve. "*Stopping learning is the same as stopping growth.*" Each experience, each challenge, and each quiet moment brings something from within. Growth is not a straight road; it's more of a pathway through valleys and mountains, where every hill you climb gets you to a new height, and once it is understood, the emphasis shifts. It changes from finishing to being present. "*Being on the journey is to embrace both the lows and highs along the way.*"

We frequently utilize the obvious indicators of accomplishment, such as the titles obtained, accolades obtained, and objectives accomplished, to gauge success. However, the more minor triumphs, the ones that aren't widely publicized or celebrated, are just as significant, if not more so. Persistence is the lifeblood of progress. It manifests in the times when you continue to move forward in the absence of others. It develops in the quiet and in the endeavor to get back up after a difficult time. Growth lacks polish and neatness. It's disorganized. It falters. Errors, detours, and days when you feel unfinished are all part of it. However, the journey's flaws are opportunities rather than indications of Failure.

Deep roots grow before branches ever stretch toward the sky. "*Growth cannot be rushed. Patience is its greatest partner.*" Slow, steady personal development may seem invisible in a world that celebrates quick wins and instant results. But it's powerful. Actual growth builds quietly, step by step, in places no one else sees. As the journey continues, transformation occurs. Who you are today won't be the same person who stands at your next milestone. "*To grow means to open ourselves to change to reinvention.*"

Over time, experience shapes us. Wisdom builds. New versions of us emerge. What matters once may change, and that's part of the process of Growth and development. You are constantly adding to what has already been done at each step. More equipped for the future, wiser from the lessons learned, and stronger by the struggle. You are continually learning, tripping, getting back up, and learning again. It's not only about completing the tasks you started. It's about the person you become while doing it.

Reaching the finish line does not lead to Growth. It is present in every action you do, including the quiet victories you achieve via introspection and hard work, the times of uncertainty you overcome, and the bravery you muster when the way seems unclear. There is no racing in this path. No end in sight. Instead, when you start to trust the process, step by step, breath by breath, something significant occurs.

REFERENCES

Jim Carrey and Manifestation: How He Used the Law of Attraction for Success. https://www.mindgrowths.com/2025/03/jim-carrey-and-manifestation-how-he.html

Navigating the Dynamic Landscape of Businesses and Entrepreneurship in Today's Fast-Paced World - tatasec.org. https://tatasec.org/navigating-the-dynamic-landscape-of-business-and-entrepreneurship-in-today-s-fast-paced-world/

Evaluating Constructability: A Key Step in Preconstruction – True North Builders. https://truenorth.builders/evaluating-constructability-a-key-step-in-preconstruction/

1199SEIU Statement on $15 Minimum Wage Deal Reached in NJ. https://www.1199seiu.org/newjersey/1199seiu-statement-15-minimum-wage-deal-reached-nj

SGP Autumn Conference - SGP. https://www.stephengeorge.co.uk/sgp-autumn-conference

Eos Price Outlook Expert Predictions for the Future. https://metaplanetofficial.com/post/eos-price-prediction/

How to deal with the fear of rejection. https://moneystepper.com/other-finance/fear-of-rejection/
https://mpelembe.net/index.php/if-there-is-systemic-inequality-why-cant-there-be-systemic-equality/?noamp=available

Navigating the Dynamic Landscape of Businesses and Entrepreneurship in Today's Fast-Paced World - tatasec.org. https://tatasec.org/navigating-the-dynamic-landscape-of-business-and-entrepreneurship-in-today-s-fast-paced-world/

Evaluating Constructability: A Key Step in Preconstruction – True North Builders. https://truenorth.builders/evaluating-constructability-a-key-step-in-preconstruction/

Overcoming Failure and Challenges | The Jōrni Blog. https://thejorniblog.com/overcoming-failure-and-challenges/

ELLE Carnival Partner: Cecil Brings Tailored Elegance And Fierce Femininity. https://elle.in/cecil-tailored-elegance-meets-fierce-femininity/

Why Mentors and Leaders Are Vital for Every Business Owner's Success. https://www.infiniteprofitconsulting.com/post/why-mentors-and-leaders-are-vital-for-every-business-owner-s-success

9 789334 238914